Chris Hadfield

INSPIRING NEW GENERATIONS TO EXPLORE SPACE

By Diane Dakers

Crabtree Publishing Company
www.crabtreebooks.com

Crabtree Publishing Company
www.crabtreebooks.com

Author: Diane Dakers
Publishing plan research and development:
  Reagan Miller
Project coordinator: Mark Sachner,
  Water Buffalo Books
Editors: Mark Sachner, Lynn Peppas
Proofreader: Wendy Scavuzzo
Indexer: Gini Holland
Editorial director: Kathy Middleton
Photo researcher: Water Buffalo Books
Designer: Westgraphix/Tammy West
**Production coordinator and prepress
  technician:** Margaret Amy Salter
Print coordinator: Margaret Amy Salter

Written, developed, and produced by
Water Buffalo Books

Publisher's note:
All quotations in this book come from original sources and
contain the spelling and grammatical inconsistencies of
the original text. Some of the quotations may also contain
terms that are no longer in use and may be considered
inappropriate or offensive. The use of such terms is for
the sake of preserving the historical and literary accuracy
of the sources and should not be seen as encouraging or
endorsing the use of such terms today.

Photographs and reproductions:
Alamy: © WENN Ltd / Alamy: p. 95 (top). **Corbis:**
© Bettmann/CORBIS: p. 22; © Dmitry Lovetsky/ /AP/Corbis
(bottom). **Getty Images:** Richard Lautens: cover (right); Clodagh
Kilcoyne: p. 60; Andrew Francis Wallace: p. 99. **NASA:** cover (left),
pp. 1, 4, 5, 7, 8, 9, 11, 13, 14, 15, 17 (top), 18 (top), 20 (top, bottom
left), 20–21 (centered bottom), 21 (second from top, bottom right),
31 (top), 32, 34, 41, 43, 44, 47, 49, 50, 51, 52, 54, 57, 59 (top), 62,
63, 65, 67, 68, 71, 73, 75, 76, 77, 78, 79, 82 (bottom), 84, 85, 87,
88, 89, 90, 94, 100, 101, 102–103, 103; NASA/Handout: cover
(inset, right background); NASA/Carla Cioffi: p. 64, 66, 80. **Public
domain:** pp. 6, 24; Captain Corey Mask: p. 36; U.S. Air Force:
pp. 37, 39. **Shutterstock:** Paul McKinnon: p. 93. **Wikipedia /
Creative Commons:** pp. 17 (bottom), 20 (second from top), 26,
31 (bottom), 55, 82 (top), 95 (bottom), 97; Hozombel at the English
language Wikipedia: p. 18 (bottom); Paul Siebert at en.wikipedia:
p. 20 (second from bottom); RIA Novosti archive, image #66514 /
Alexander Mokletsov / CC-BY-SA 3.0: p. 21 (top).

Cover: Foreground: While aboard the International Space
Station (ISS) between December 2012 and May 2013, astronaut
Chris Hadfield became the first Canadian to lead an ISS mission.
Background: He also built up a powerful social media presence,
tweeting, telling stories, singing songs, and beaming back to Earth
thousands of photos with captivating descriptions. Here, Chris
is shown on a large screen, playing his guitar and singing with
school kids via a video link.

Library and Archives Canada Cataloguing in Publication

Dakers, Diane, author
       Chris Hadfield : inspiring new generations to explore space
/ Diane Dakers.

(Crabtree groundbreaker biographies)
Includes index.
Issued in print and electronic formats.
ISBN 978-0-7787-2558-9 (bound).--ISBN 978-0-7787-2560-2
(paperback).--ISBN 978-1-4271-9990-4 (pdf).--ISBN 978-1-4271-
9988-1 (html)

       1. Hadfield, Chris, 1959- --Juvenile literature. 2.
Astronauts--Canada--Biography--Juvenile literature. 3.
Astronautics--Juvenile literature. I. Title. II. Series: Crabtree
groundbreaker biographies

TL789.85.H34D35 2015   j629.450092   C2015-903383-7
                                          C2015-903384-5

Library of Congress Cataloging-in-Publication Data

Dakers, Diane.
  Chris Hadfield : inspiring new generations to explore space / Diane
Dakers.
       pages cm. -- (Crabtree groundbreaker biographies)
  Includes index.
  ISBN 978-0-7787-2558-9 (reinforced library binding) -- ISBN 978-
0-7787-2560-2 (pbk.) -- ISBN 978-1-4271-9990-4 (electronic pdf)
-- ISBN 978-1-4271-9988-1 (electronic html)
  1. Hadfield, Chris, 1959---Juvenile literature. 2. Astronauts--
Canada--Biography--Juvenile literature. I. Title.

TL789.85.H34D34 2016
629.450092--dc23
[B]
                                          2015022180

Crabtree Publishing Company
www.crabtreebooks.com   1-800-387-7650   Printed in Canada/102015/IH20150821

**Published
in Canada
Crabtree Publishing**
616 Welland Ave.
St. Catharines, Ontario
L2M 5V6

**Published in
the United States
Crabtree Publishing**
PMB 59051
350 Fifth Ave., 59th Floor
New York, NY 10118

**Published in the
United Kingdom
Crabtree Publishing**
Maritime House
Basin Road North, Hove
BN41 1WR

**Published
in Australia
Crabtree Publishing**
3 Charles Street
Coburg North
VIC, 3058

Contents

Chapter 1
Big Dreams

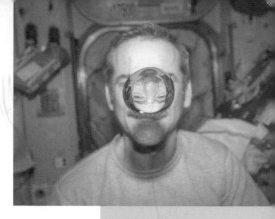

On Sunday, July 20, 1969, U.S. astronaut Neil Armstrong stepped out of his lunar module, climbed down a short ladder, and stepped onto the dusty ground. With that, he became the first human in history to set foot on the Moon. Twenty minutes later, his colleague Buzz Aldrin joined him on the celestial surface. About 600 million people around the world were glued to their televisions that day, watching the historic event. One of those viewers was a nine-year-old boy named Chris Hadfield.

Astronaut Chris Hadfield demonstrates the effects of zero gravity on a water bubble floating in front of him on the International Space Station in January 2013. Light is refracted, or made to change direction, by the bubble, so his face appears upside down.

Opposite: One of the space program's most energetic and creative personalities, Chris Hadfield is shown (top) in a NASA portrait with the flags of Canada and the United States. Once aboard the International Space Station (ISS), he showed a less formal side, engaging school kids in experiments and other programs, and displaying a range of activities and observations that made him a social-media favorite back on Earth. Here (bottom), in March 2013, he demonstrates the effects of zero gravity as he takes a break from his duties as ISS commander. He has donned a green sweater, shirt, and bow tie in honor of St. Patrick's Day.

A girl holds a copy of The Washington Post *on the day after the historic July 20, 1969, Apollo 11 Moon landing. The event fueled the imaginations of hundreds of millions of people around the world, including a young Canadian named Chris Hadfield.*

Future Astronaut

On that summer night, young Chris decided that he, too, would become an astronaut. "I was inspired by them," he said many years later. "I not only wanted to be an astronaut, I wanted to be Neil Armstrong. He was pretty cool."

The problem for Chris, though, was that he was Canadian—and Canada didn't have a space program. But that wasn't going to stop this determined youngster. From that day forward,

HADFIELD'S HEROES

To nine-year-old Chris Hadfield, astronauts Neil Armstrong and Buzz Aldrin were idols. They inspired him. He wanted to follow in their footsteps. He became an astronaut because of them.

Neil Armstrong was born in 1930. He was an officer in the U.S. Navy, and flew combat missions as a pilot in the Korean War in 1951–1952. He then worked as a test pilot before becoming an astronaut in 1962. He made his first spaceflight in 1966, then served as commander of the Apollo 11 Moon mission three years later. He resigned from NASA in 1971 and became a university professor. He died at age 82 in 2012.

Buzz Aldrin was born in 1930 and had a military career before becoming an astronaut. He also served as a fighter pilot in the Korean War. He became an astronaut in 1963, making his first spaceflight three years later. He joined Neil Armstrong on the Moon in July 1969. He retired from NASA in 1971, and from the military a year later. Since then, he has written a number of books and appeared in movies, TV shows, and a rap music video. He competed on *Dancing with the Stars* in 2010.

Test pilot Neil Armstrong stands beside the rocket-powered X-15 after a flight in November 1959, nearly ten years before his historic flight to the Moon and back. The experimental craft was capable of flying at speeds of over 4,500 miles per hour (7,242 kilometers per hour). It could fly at altitudes that brought the plane to the edge of outer space and created the condition of weightlessness inside the cockpit. It's no wonder the X-15 was used to qualify pilots for astronaut status and bring back valuable data about space flight.

he started living his life as a future astronaut.

Chris researched American astronauts to find out what kinds of things they had in common. What sort of education did they have? What jobs did they do before they became astronauts? What kind of people were they? What did they do in their spare time?

Whatever astronauts had done in their early lives, that's what Chris did.

One thing he learned was that all the astronauts in the space program at the time had started out as fighter pilots. So that became Chris's first goal, sending him on his own personal flight path.

At 13, Chris became an Air Cadet. At 15, he qualified as a glider pilot, earning his power pilot license a year later. He joined the military at 18 and became a fighter pilot when he was 25. He had reached the first major milestone in his

MISSION ACCOMPLISHED

The goal of the Apollo 11 mission was simple: "Perform a manned lunar landing and return." The eight-day mission, July 16–24, 1969, did just that.

After it launched from the Kennedy Space Center in Florida, the Apollo 11 craft took three days to enter its orbit around the Moon. The following day, the lunar module, called *Eagle*, touched down on the Moon's surface. It remained there for 21 hours.

During that time, two astronauts—Neil Armstrong and Buzz Aldrin—became the first humans to set foot on the Moon. A third astronaut, Michael Collins, piloted the main spacecraft in orbit around the Moon until *Eagle* returned to it.

Armstrong and Aldrin spent about two and a half hours walking on the Moon. During their moonwalk, they placed a plaque, planted flags (which they then took home), took photos, and collected rock samples for study on Earth.

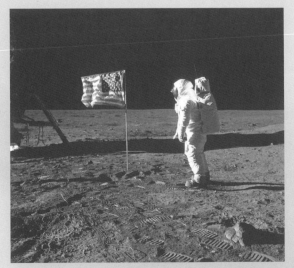

Above: The Apollo 11 crew—Collins, Armstrong, and Aldrin—in front of a mock-up of the lunar module about a month before their journey to the Moon.

Buzz Aldrin salutes the U.S. flag that he has just planted on the Moon. Since there is no wind on the lunar surface, the flag was designed with ripples to make it look as though it was blowing in the breeze.

plan to become an astronaut.

What was even better was that, by then, Canada had launched its own space program. That meant Chris had a shot at turning his dream into a reality. He wasn't ready when the first group of astronauts was hired, but his turn came nine years later.

In 1992, after a grueling application process, Chris was selected—out of more than 5,300 applicants—as one of four new Canadian astronauts. Twenty-three years after watching the historic Moon landing, his childhood dream had come true!

Since then, Chris has flown on three different space missions. He was also the voice of Mission Control, the person on the ground who communicated with astronauts in orbit, for 25 space shuttle flights. In 2001, Chris became the first Canadian to walk in space, and in 2013, he was the first Canadian ever appointed as commander of the International Space Station (ISS).

Reaching for the Stars

While Chris was flying on the ISS, he became a superstar back here on Earth. For five months, he used Twitter, Reddit, SoundCloud, Tumblr, and Facebook, as well as videos posted on YouTube, to share his experiences with millions of earthbound fans.

Practically everything he did went viral because, even though Chris was living an out-of-this-world life, "he came off as a regular guy tweeting to friends about his day," wrote *Forbes* magazine. "He sold us on the mystical, beautiful, transformational experience he was having on

Chris Hadfield during a live interview from the ISS, as he unveils the new Canadian five-dollar bill. The bill can be seen floating next to Chris's right shoulder.

his trip through space." He brought his fellow Earthlings along for the ride.

He tweeted hundreds of photos, sang songs, and recorded videos showing how simple things became difficult—or funny—in zero gravity. He unveiled Canada's new five-dollar bill from space. He answered questions, conducted experiments, and sang, live via video link, with school kids.

During one press conference, he also told us about the one thing he didn't like on the ISS. "The only thing that gets me mad is I have to sleep," he said just after he took command of the ship. "My resolution has been to make the absolute most of [this trip]—to spend as little time sleeping as I can."

By the time Chris came back down to Earth,

> "A lot of people think that astronauts, their job is about flying in space. I was an astronaut for 21 years, and I was in space for six months. The reality of an astronaut's job is all about being on Earth and preparing and helping other people fly in space.... There's a huge amount of work that happens on Earth in order to make the very rare experience of space travel happen."
>
> Chris Hadfield

the whole world had caught Hadfield fever, something that continued long after his landing. Today, Chris may no longer be soaring in the skies, but his star continues to shine.

He draws a crowd everywhere he goes, whether he's singing in Canada's capital city of Ottawa, delivering a lecture at the university where he now teaches, or signing copies of the two books he has published since landing.

Throughout his career, Chris has been honored with numerous awards and medals. He earned NASA's Exceptional Service Medal in 2002, the Queen's Golden and Diamond Jubilee medals in 2002 and 2012, and two Meritorious Service Crosses from the Canadian military. He is in Canada's Aviation Hall of Fame. His face is stamped on gold and silver commemorative coins. He holds honorary degrees and diplomas from colleges and universities across Canada.

There are three Chris Hadfield Public Schools

Gimme an "A"

When he first stepped onto the surface of the Moon, Neil Armstrong planned to say, "That's one small step for *a* man, one giant leap for mankind." What billions of TV viewers around the world heard was the same sentence without the "a": "That's one small step for man, one giant leap for mankind." Traditionally, "man" has been a synonym for "mankind"—or, in today's terms, "humankind" or "humanity." So, without the "a," the sentence might mean, "That's one small step for mankind, one giant leap for mankind." This would seem nonsensical and ruin the intended effect of Armstrong's statement!

For years, Armstrong insisted he had said "*a* man." In 1999, however, even he admitted he couldn't hear the "a" on the famous recording, and after listening to it at various speeds, he is reported to have said with a sigh, "Damn. I really did it. I blew the first words on the Moon, didn't I?"

Over the last few years, however, several theories have emerged to support the possibility that Armstrong had indeed said "for *a* man." One is from a computer expert who claimed to have analyzed the tape and discovered "a 35-millisecond-long bump of sound between 'for' and 'man' that would have been too brief for human ears to hear." Another is from researchers who have studied the speech patterns of people from around Armstrong's hometown in Ohio. They have found that often "for" and "a" are pushed together, creating a sound like "frruh."

You can listen for yourself and decide:

http://www.nasa.gov/62284main_onesmall2.wav

Perhaps more important than what you hear (or want to hear) is the fact that Armstrong's words are one of the best-known, if most debated, quotes in history.

Neil Armstrong takes his first step onto the surface of the Moon. In a few seconds, Armstrong would describe this moment with words that have become among the most famous, and debated, quotations in recent history. This image was taken from a grainy TV broadcast beamed to Earth by a camera mounted on the lunar module.

The weightless environment aboard the ISS allows Chris Hadfield to effortlessly juggle a batch of tomatoes ferried up from Earth aboard a cargo spacecraft in 2013.

in southern Ontario. Chris's former Air Cadet Squadron, formerly called 820 Milton Blue Thunder, is now called 820 Chris Hadfield Squadron. He also has an asteroid named after him: Asteroid 14143 Hadfield.

He has been honored for his photography, his outreach work, and his musical entertainment abilities. On Canada Day, July 1, 2014, he and his brother Dave released what they called "the most Canadian music video ever made." The song, titled "In Canada," has been viewed on YouTube more than 1.6 million times.

Just like the tune, "a polite song from two brothers who are just hoping your day is going OK," Chris is now known around the world. Despite that international spotlight, though, and like the song, Chris is Canadian through and through, a down-to-Earth farm kid who had a big dream.

> *"I have been one of the luckiest guys on Earth."*
>
> Chris Hadfield

WHY SPEND THE MONEY?

One of Chris's personal and professional missions as an astronaut was to convince Canadians that exploring space is still important—despite how much it costs.

"I don't want to waste other people's money just so I can go for a ride," he said. "As much fun as it is, that's not the point."

The point of space travel, he says, is to learn about Earth by observing it from above. It's also about the learning we gain from the hundreds of scientific experiments astronauts conduct on the ISS every year. The knowledge gained in space might help us live better, healthier lives on Earth.

Humans have always wanted to know what is beyond the world they can see. That's simple human nature. Early explorers traveled by wooden ships to reach continents and other places they never imagined existed. Today's space explorers use current technology to reach beyond Earthly borders. The goal is to learn more about the universe and humanity's place in it.

Chris believes space travel is also important because it inspires future generations. "You have to provide your children with a challenge that is right on the edge of impossible in order for a nation and a culture to grow."

NASA astronaut Karen Nyberg performs an eye exam on herself aboard the International Space Station in 2013. The vacuum of space outside the station and zero gravity within create research opportunities and laboratory conditions unlike anything on planet Earth.

Chapter 2
From Farm Boy to Fly Boy

A corn farm in southwestern Ontario, Canada, may not seem like the obvious training ground for a future astronaut. But it *is* a place where a kid can learn the value of hard work, while being surrounded by space to dream. A corn farm is exactly where Canada's most famous astronaut got his start.

Down on the Farm

Christopher Austin Hadfield was born on August 29, 1959, in Sarnia, Ontario, an industrial town at the southern tip of Lake Huron. He was the second of five children—three sons and two daughters—to Roger, a pilot and flight instructor, and Eleanor, a homemaker.

Sarnia, Ontario. Chris Hadfield spent the first seven years of his life in this town. Perched at the southernmost point of Lake Huron, it is on the Canadian side of the St. Clair River, right across from Port Huron, Michigan, on the U.S. side.

When Chris was seven years old, his dad got a job with Air Canada, one of the country's largest passenger airlines. Roger was then flying in and out of Toronto International Airport, a long way from Sarnia.

That meant the family had to move. In 1967, Eleanor and Roger chose the town of Milton, about 150 miles (240 km) east of Sarnia, as their new home. "My parents bought a farm," remembered Chris. "Both of them had grown up on farms and viewed [the move] as a wonderful opportunity to work themselves to the bone while carrying on the family tradition." The farm was only a half-hour drive from the airport, where Chris's dad reported for his flight duties.

Bottom: Downtown Milton, Ontario—the town Chris Hadfield grew up in as a young boy and teenager. Top: A photo of Milton taken by Chris in March 2013 from the International Space Station. Here is the caption he wrote: "Milton, Ontario, where I grew up. Looking closely I can see my parents' farm—and Chris Hadfield Public School!"

The farm was also a place where Chris and his brothers and sisters had plenty of room to play and explore their own interests—after they had finished their chores, of course. Chris learned how to drive a tractor, harvest crops, and fix things when they broke. He learned independence, patience, and how to challenge himself.

When Chris was still a toddler, his parents bought a cottage on Stag Island, a few miles south of Sarnia. The family spent summers there throughout Chris's childhood. Today, his parents still own the cottage and still spend time there every summer.

That's where the family was on July 20, 1969—the day young Chris watched the Apollo 11 Moon landing on a neighbor's TV. "The image was grainy, but I knew exactly what we were seeing: the impossible, made possible," wrote Chris in his 2013 book *An Astronaut's Guide to Life on Earth*. "Later," he wrote,

> "... *walking back to our cottage, I looked up at the Moon. It was no longer a distant, unknowable orb but a place where people walked, talked, worked and even slept. At that moment, I knew what I wanted to do with my life.*"

Chris knew, though, that the odds were against him ever reaching this dream. At the time, Canada didn't even have a space agency. Everyone knew that "astronauts were American," he said.

Sputnik 1

Explorer 1

Yuri Gagarin

Alan Shepard

THE SPACE RACE

In the 1950s and 1960s, the attention of people around the world, including a boy named Chris Hadfield, was riveted by an international race to outer space. Two nations were on a mission to become the leader in space flight.

What came to be called "the space race" began in the summer of 1955 when the Soviet Union and the United States both announced their plans to launch satellites into orbit. Each nation wanted to prove its technological, military, and political superiority over the other.

On October 4, 1957, the Soviet Union won the first leg of the race when it launched the first-ever artificial satellite to go into orbit around Earth. The satellite, called *Sputnik 1*, was a 23-inch (58-centimeter) wide shiny sphere, about the size of a beach ball. A month later, *Sputnik 2* took off, this time with a little dog named Laika on board.

It would be another three months before the United States sent its first satellite, *Explorer 1*, into orbit.

In 1961, the Soviet Union took another leap forward in the space race when cosmonaut Yuri Gagarin became the first human in space. Three weeks later, astronaut Alan Shepard became the first American in space.

In 1963, the Soviets again made headlines when they sent the first woman, Valentina Tereshkova, into space. It would be 20 years (1983) before Sally Ride, the first U.S. woman in space, took to the skies.

In the mid-1960s, the players in the space race turned their attention to the Moon. This time, the Americans won. On July 20, 1969, U.S. Apollo 11 astronauts Neil Armstrong, Buzz

Aldrin, and Michael Collins put their craft into lunar orbit, and Armstrong and Aldrin became the first humans to set foot on the Moon. Between 1969 and 1972, the United States launched a total of six lunar missions resulting in astronauts walking on the Moon.

The Soviet Union never put a human on the Moon. Having lost the race to the Moon, the Soviets focused on other types of space technology and exploration. These included unmanned probes and manned, Earth-orbiting space stations.

The space race began to wind down in 1972, when the United States and the Soviet Union agreed to work together in outer space. As part of that agreement, the two nations sent crews into space on a joint U.S.–Soviet space flight in 1975. This mission, which involved the docking of a U.S. Apollo and a Soviet Soyuz craft, was the first time U.S. and Soviet crews had worked together in space. It marked the end of the space race and paved the way for future joint missions such as the shuttle-*Mir* program and the International Space Station.

Valentina Tereshkova

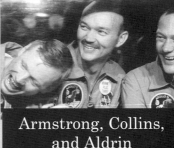

Sally Ride

Armstrong, Collins, and Aldrin

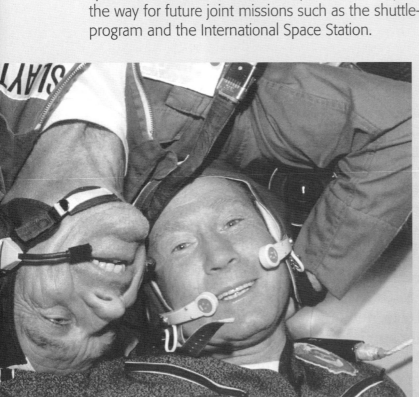

U.S. astronaut Donald K. "Deke" Slayton and Soviet cosmonaut Aleksey A. Leonov during the joint Apollo-Soyuz mission in 1975. The mission marked the end of the U.S.–Soviet space race.

SPACE ON THE SCREEN

In the late 1960s, two space-age shows captured young Chris Hadfield's attention and started him thinking about going where no Canadian had gone before.

One was a 1968 movie called *2001: A Space Odyssey*. Considered by some people to be the greatest sci-fi movie of all time, *2001* is a complicated story that is based on a fictional discovery on the Moon in 1999 that leads to a voyage to Jupiter in 2001.

A small-screen show also sparked Chris's passion for outer space. The original *Star Trek* series (1966–1969) aired on TV during the time leading up to, and after, Neil Armstrong and Buzz Aldrin's first steps on the Moon. The original *Star Trek* led to four spin-off television series, an animated TV series, and 12 feature films, with another movie set for a 2016 release.

Leonard Nimoy as Science/First Officer Mr. Spock (left) and William Shatner as Capt. James T. Kirk in a 1968 publicity photo for the original TV series Star Trek. *Also shown is a model of the starship* Enterprise, *the legendary spacecraft that was the setting for all the* Star Trek *TV episodes and movies featuring Kirk and Spock.*

> *"The sky is not the limit. You are the result of your day-to-day decisions, and it's amazing where those decisions can take you. What you do today turns you into who you are tomorrow."*
>
> Chris Hadfield, July 2014

learn. They learned problem-solving skills. They learned to question everything. These were skills that Chris-the-future-astronaut would need!

In the fall of 1972, when he was 13, Chris joined Air Cadets, which he described as "sort of a cross between Boy Scouts and the Air Force." There, he developed even more skills required for a career in space—leadership, responsibility, and self-discipline. He also learned how to fly.

In 1975, at the age of 15, Chris became a glider pilot. A glider is an airplane that has no engine. Gliders are towed into the sky, then released to soar silently and gracefully back to Earth.

A year later, in the summer of 1976, Chris earned his license to fly engine-powered planes. He was a pilot—and he was only 16 years old!

"I loved the sensation, the speed, the challenge of trying to execute maneuvers with some degree of elegance," he wrote years later. "I loved flying."

That wasn't the only thing the teenager loved. He loved skiing, particularly downhill racing. He became a ski racer and instructor while he was still in high school. "Skiing all day was a

A sailplane/glider used in the glider training program of the Royal Canadian Air Cadets. The plane bears an Air Cadets ID and is painted in its color scheme.

THE HIGH-FLYING HADFIELDS

Chris Hadfield isn't the only member of his family to take to the skies. His father Roger was the first pilot ever to land a plane at the Sarnia Airport. He was also a flight instructor there before becoming a captain with Air Canada. Chris's older brother David started his aviation career as a baggage handler. He is now a pilot with Air Canada, so is younger brother Phillip. David's wife, Robin, is also a pilot, and the couple's son Austin (Chris's nephew) also flies for Air Canada.

Chris's younger sisters, Anna Jean and Patricia, joined Air Cadets when they were teenagers, but they did not become pilots.

ridiculously fun way to make money."

Chris loved swimming, waterskiing, and canoeing at the family cottage. He also loved music—a passion he inherited from his parents. He played guitar with his brother, played trombone in the high school band, and sang in the school choir.

As much as he enjoyed these other activities, though, Chris never lost sight of his dream to become an astronaut. So, as his high school years came to a close, he asked himself what an astronaut would do after graduation.

The answer he came up with was to join the military.

FAMILY MAN

When Chris Hadfield was in high school, he dabbled in drama, playing a role in a production of *The Man Who Came to Dinner*. A girl named Helene Walter was also involved in the play.

In 1977, after rehearsal one day, Chris offered Helene a ride home. "I took a ride home, and that was that," she said. "We were dating."

Four years later, just before Christmas 1981, Chris and Helene got married. He was still in college, and she worked in an insurance agency. Within six years, the couple had three children—Kyle, Evan, and Kristin.

Today, Kyle lives in China, Evan in Germany, and Kristin in Ireland.

A Career Takes Off

In Canada, there are two ways to begin a military career. One is to simply sign up for the Canadian Armed Forces, and to serve in an entry-level position with the army, navy, or air force. The other way is to attend military college, to prepare for a specific career within the Armed Forces.

Chris chose the educational route, attending military college for four years (1978–1982), first at Royal Roads Military College in Victoria, British Columbia, then at Royal Military College in Kingston, Ontario.

During his college years, he also completed basic military flight training, finishing as top pilot in his class.

Chris graduated in 1982 with a bachelor's degree in mechanical engineering. "I figured ... the odds of being an astronaut are pretty lousy,

CLASS OF 1980

From *The Log*, the Royal Roads
Military College Yearbook, 1980:

Hadfield, C. A.

*"Chris arrived at Roads as a country hick,
staring in awe at the big city. His farmboy
brains and brawn enabled him to survive first
year unscathed.*

*"During his second year, Chris kept busy....
When not pursuing his insatiable appetite
for knowledge, Chris could be found racing
up and against the mountains with the 500
club, or racing down them with the ski club. In
his spare time, Chris survived drowning as a
member of the RRMC waterpolo team.*

*"Next year, Chris plans to go to RMC in
Kingston. There he will major in Mechanical
Engineering and Anatomy. Helene is quite
pleased with his choice of courses.*

*"Chris ... hopes to be a fighter pilot while there
are still planes to fly. Best of luck to you Chris
and remember the ejector button."*

and I need something else as a real career."

If the astronaut dream didn't work out,
he knew he could be happy spending his life
working as an engineer. If that astronaut dream
was going to work out, though, Chris knew he
had to fly even higher.

Chapter 3
Ready to Launch

By the time he finished his university education, Chris Hadfield was an accomplished pilot. But he knew that, to become an astronaut, he would need even more skills in the sky. A year after graduation, he took a Basic Jet Training program. As usual, he aced his courses, finishing as the top student in his class. Chris wasn't just aiming for the skies, though. He was reaching for the stars. He had to fly farther, faster, and higher.

School in the Sky

In 1983, when Chris was 24 years old, an incredible thing happened. The Canadian government hired its first-ever astronauts. With that, Chris's impossible dream suddenly became, in his words, "marginally more possible."

At that point, Chris became even more focused on his future. He was on the right path, and now that path might actually take him where he had always wanted to go!

In jet flight school, Chris spent 200 hours in a CT-114 Tutor. That is the aircraft used by the Royal Canadian Air Force aerobatic team, the Snowbirds.

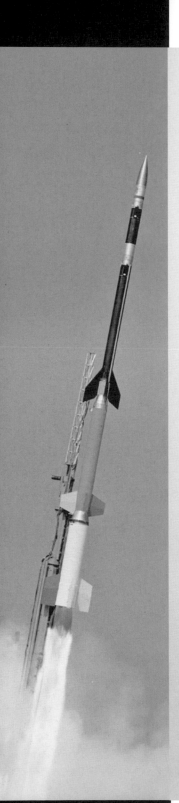

Launching **NASA** and the **CSA**

On October 1, 1958, the United States launched NASA—the National Aeronautics and Space Administration. That was during the "space race," when the United States was competing with the Soviet Union to be the first to reach outer space. Before NASA, the United States had been involved in developing rockets for military purposes, but NASA was to be a civilian space agency. Its goal was—and is—to promote peaceful space programs. NASA oversees all U.S. space exploration, research, science, and technology. It also partners with agencies from other nations in the peaceful exploration of space.

In 1983, the United States invited Canada to send an astronaut on one of NASA's space shuttle missions. At the time, Canada didn't have a space program. It created one that year, however, through the National Research Council of Canada, the country's science-and-technology branch. Immediately, the newly formed Canadian Astronaut Program set out to recruit six astronauts.

Six years later, the government of Canada created an independent organization to deal with everything space-related in the country. Since 1989, the Canadian Space Agency (CSA) has overseen the nation's role in space science and exploration, satellite communications, space awareness, and astronaut selection.

Black Brant rockets have been a major contribution of Canadian technology and engineering to both NASA and the CSA. Since their development in the 1950s, they have been among the most popular rockets used for upper-atmosphere and sub-orbital research.

The next logical step in his self-designed astronaut-preparation program was to become a fighter pilot—so Chris embarked on a year-long fighter-jet-training course.

Upon completion, he was assigned to a flight squadron at Canadian Forces Base (CFB) Bagotville, in the province of Quebec. As part of its duties for NORAD—the North American Aerospace Defense Command—the squadron's role was to protect Canadian airspace.

On his first day on the job with 425 Squadron, Chris made fighter pilot history. In his own words:

"At that time the Soviets were flying their long-range bombers into Canadian airspace for a couple of reasons. Sometimes they took shortcuts through Canada on their way to Cuba. Other times they came to practice their cruise missile launches on North America."

His squadron's job was to stop the Soviets from doing that.

High-Risk Business

On Chris's first night with the squadron, in June 1985, a group of Soviet bombers entered the airspace over northeastern Canada. His squadron was ordered into the skies to intercept them, or head them off. As Chris neared the foreign aircraft, he could hear the hum of their engines in the darkness. He turned on his searchlights and caught sight of the Soviet planes. Keeping his lights trained on the bombers, he stayed with them until they left Canadian airspace.

Canada's First Astronauts

In 1983, Canada recruited its first astronauts through the Canadian Astronaut Program. More than 4,000 people applied, and six were selected:

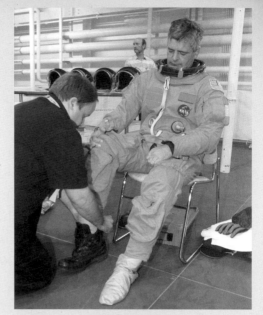

- Marc Garneau was the first Canadian in space (1984) and the first Canadian to make a second visit to space (1996). He was president of the Canadian Space Agency from 2001 to 2005, the year he retired from the CSA.
- Roberta Bondar was the first Canadian woman in space (1992). She left the space program later that year.
- Steve MacLean visited space twice (1992, 2006), and he was the second Canadian (after Chris Hadfield) to do a spacewalk. He served as CSA president, 2008–2013, retiring in 2013.
- Robert Thirsk visited space twice (1996, 2009), and holds the Canadian record for most time spent in space (204 days). He retired from the CSA in 2012.
- Bjarni Tryggvason visited space in 1997. He worked on many other projects within the CSA until his retirement in 2008.
- Kenneth Money served as alternate astronaut on a 1992 mission, but never flew in space. He retired from the Canadian Astronaut Corps in 1992.

Top to bottom: Marc Garneau, the first Canadian in space; Roberta Bondar, the first Canadian woman in space; Steve MacLean, the second Canadian to do a spacewalk.

It was the first time a CF-18 pilot had ever intercepted Soviet "Bear" bombers and escorted them out of Canadian airspace. "It was important," Chris said later. "Not that they were going to launch their missiles and not that we were going to do anything hostile, but to demonstrate the ability to defend ourselves, to demonstrate that we know what is going on within our borders."

While he was posted to CFB Bagotville, Chris began to question his astronaut dream for the first time in his life. His career as a fighter pilot was hard on his family. He and his wife Helene had two children, Kyle and Evan, and a baby on the way. They were struggling financially. Chris's foreseeable future was filled with hard work, poor pay, and high risk.

"Aside from anything else, being a fighter pilot is dangerous," he said. "We were losing at least one close friend every year" to flight accidents.

Around that time, Air Canada announced it was hiring new pilots. Chris considered a career move. "Working for an airline would be an easier life for us," he said.

Luckily, Helene talked some sense into her husband. "You don't really want to be an airline pilot," she told him. "You wouldn't be happy and then I wouldn't be happy. Don't give up on being an astronaut—I can't let you do that to yourself or to us. Let's wait just a little bit longer and see how things play out."

As it happened, things were to play out quite nicely for Chris.

A Canadian CF-18 Hornet (lower) escorts a U.S. Air Force B-52 during a joint Canadian–U.S. NORAD training exercise.

PROTECTING THE SKIES

In the 1980s, Chris Hadfield was a member of 425 Tactical Fighter Squadron, which was (and still is) part of the North American Aerospace Defense Command (NORAD).

Founded in 1957, NORAD brings together the armed forces of Canada and the United States in a mission to protect the airspace over the two nations. It provides warning and defense systems against unwelcome aircraft.

Today NORAD is divided into three regions—the Alaskan, Canadian, and Continental U.S. Regions. Each has its own headquarters and commander.

On Christmas Eve, NORAD tracks, photographs, and escorts Santa Claus as he completes his mission to deliver toys to children all around the world.

Testing, Testing

As much as Chris loved flying, he also loved learning about the inner workings of aircraft. He was an engineer, after all!

"As a fighter pilot, I helped defend North America by using the latest aerospace technology," he said. "But... I wanted to then get into aircraft design and testing."

He wanted to use his mechanical engineering skills to help make high-performance planes faster, more fuel efficient, and safer. He wanted to push aircraft to their limits to discover ways to improve them.

While he was still part of 425 Squadron, Chris started to get "a tiny taste" of this type of work. He began to volunteer to be the first to fly airplanes coming out of the maintenance shop— to be the test pilot on the base. "I was hooked." He decided that test pilot school would be his next stop.

"People on the squadron were genuinely puzzled when I said I wanted to go to test pilot school. Why would anyone give up the glory of

A Soviet Tu-95 "Bear" aircraft is intercepted by a Canadian CF-18 in 1987. About two years earlier, Chris Hadfield had become the first CF-18 pilot to escort a Bear bomber out of Canadian airspace.

being a fighter pilot to be an engineer, essentially? But the engineering aspects of the job were exactly what appealed to me."

However, just as Canada had no astronaut program when Chris decided he wanted to become an astronaut, it had no test pilot school when he decided to become a test pilot.

Fortunately, every year, the Canadian Armed Forces selected two pilots to study at flight schools in other countries.

In 1987, Chris was one of those chosen. He jumped at the chance to attend the U.S. Air Force Test Pilot School at Edwards Air Force Base in California.

"Test pilot school was like getting a Ph.D. in flying," he said. "In a single year, we flew 32 different types of planes and were tested every day. It was incredibly tough—and incredibly fun."

He enjoyed the camaraderie, or friendship, of the group of like-minded individuals. They were all about the same age. They all loved the math, science, and problem solving of flying. And most of them wanted to become astronauts.

As usual, come graduation time, Chris was the top student in his class. "I took some nationalistic pride in it too—a Canadian, the top U.S. Air Force test pilot graduate!"

Becoming an astronaut was still a long shot, but Chris now had *another* career to fall back on if need be. "I knew I'd feel I was doing something worthwhile with my life if I spent the rest of it as a test pilot."

The Final Step in Astronaut Prep

Shortly after graduation from test pilot school, Chris was posted to Patuxent River Naval Air Station in Maryland. There, as part of a Canadian exchange program, he flew F-18s and A-7s with the U.S. Navy. Finally, he was a full-fledged test pilot, blending his love of flying with his engineering interests.

It was a dangerous job that demanded Chris push to the limits of the abilities of his aircraft, and himself. "Trying to make airplanes that could fly where airplanes could never fly before ... was really interesting to me, and it was risky," he said. "But... some things are worth taking a risk for."

The main building of the U.S. Air Force Test Pilot School at Edwards Air Force Base.

> *"Chris always knew that to get where he wanted to go, he had to be the best. So he was always the best at what he did."*
>
> Roger Hadfield,
> Chris's dad, 2012

Chris and his family spent three years at Pax, as the base was commonly called. He loved his job, but his head was still in outer space. Once again, he asked himself what else he could do to make sure he was ready to become an astronaut if the opportunity ever arose.

One thing he didn't have was an advanced university degree, something that all astronauts had. So earning a graduate degree became Chris's new goal.

While he worked by day at Pax, he spent evenings and weekends working on a degree in aviation systems at the University of Tennessee. He completed the program through distance education, and in 1992 he graduated with a Master of Science degree in aviation systems.

Meanwhile, he won two more awards—a research award from the Society of Experimental Test Pilots and the U.S. Navy's 1991 Test Pilot of the Year Award.

By this time, Chris's posting at Pax was drawing to a close, and all the pieces of his astronaut preparation plan were in place. He decided he deserved a bit of downtime. "My plan was to relax a bit and enjoy our final year [at Pax], spend more time with the kids and play a little more guitar."

"Where's Chris?" His mustache and his guitar make Chris Hadfield easy to spot as he joins fellow crew members for a brief Christmas celebration aboard the International Space Station in December 2012.

MUSTACHIO MAN

Sure, Chris Hadfield is world-renowned for being an astronaut. But he's just as famous for his world-class 'stache!

The future spaceman started growing his trademark upper-lip frizz when he turned 18. "I decided 'I'm 18, I'm a man, I'm going to grow a moustache,' " he said.

Chris has only shaved off his mo' once since then. It was when he was in test pilot school. The U.S. Air Force frowns on 'staches, said Chris. So he shaved it off.

Nobody—especially his wife Helene—liked the look of bald-faced Chris. "So that's why I have a moustache."

Chris isn't the only mustachioed man famous for his facial hair. Here are a few more: scientist Albert Einstein, artist Salvador Dali, actor Tom Selleck, comedian Groucho Marx, dictator Adolf Hitler, and cartoon outlaw Yosemite Sam.

Chapter 4
The Right Stuff

When Chris Hadfield answered the Canadian Space Agency's help-wanted ad, he wasn't alone. Exactly 5,329 other candidates also hoped to become astronauts. To make sure he was chosen, Chris spent 10 days preparing his application package. He included two versions—one in each of Canada's official languages, English and French. He had it professionally printed and bound. He proofread it so many times that he even began editing in his dreams while he slept. Finally, he couriered the precious parcel to the Canadian Space Agency in Ottawa. Then he waited.

Making the Cut

Week after nail-biting week passed before Chris heard back from the CSA about his astronaut application. When he finally got word, it was great news! He had made it to the next round of the recruitment process—along with 499 other candidates.

The next step was to fill out more forms, complete with a psychological evaluation. Then more waiting. It was another month before Chris learned he had made the next cut. He was now in the top 100!

> *"I wondered whether this whole process was in fact a cunningly designed stress test to see how applicants coped with uncertainty and irritation."*
>
> Chris Hadfield, referring to the astronaut-hiring process

So You Wanna Be an Astronaut...

Astronauts come from a variety of backgrounds, but they all have a few things in common. NASA and the CSA have similar requirements for their high-flying recruits.

To be considered for astronaut-hood, you must have a university degree (a graduate degree is even better) in engineering, science, or math—or you must be a licensed medical doctor. You must be healthy and fit, with good eyesight, keen hearing, and healthy blood pressure. You must be a team player and a problem solver, and qualify for high security clearance. A love of travel and a passion for floating in zero gravity also help!

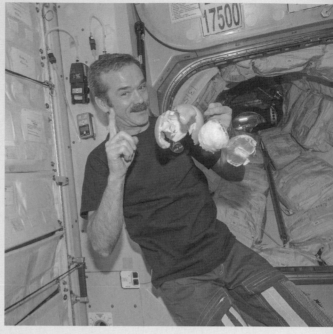

Got grapefruit? As his many social-media fans know, Chris Hadfield is happy to demonstrate an essential ingredient for being an astronaut: his passion for zero gravity!

From there, the hiring process only got tougher. Next up was an interview with a psychologist in Washington, D.C., and more weeks of waiting. Again, Chris made it through to the next round. He was now one of 50 finalists for the astro-jobs. For the first time, he allowed himself to believe that his dream of becoming an astronaut might *actually* come true!

The next set of interviews and tests for the astronaut hopefuls took place in Toronto. "It was horribly nerve-wracking," Chris recalled. "Then I made the final round. Twenty candidates were being summoned to Ottawa."

There, the final few underwent medical examinations, interviews, and public relations exercises to see who among them had the right stuff. At the end of the week, "I had no idea whether they liked me more or less than anyone else," said Chris. He went home "having no clue whether they were going to choose me or not."

A few more anxious weeks passed. Finally, one Saturday in May 1992, five months after

What Is "the Right Stuff"?

"The right stuff," the title of a 1979 book by Tom Wolfe, is a phrase that has come to mean having what it takes to be an astronaut. The phrase became even better known with the release, in 1983, of a popular movie based on Wolfe's book.

The Right Stuff is the story of the first 15 years of NASA's space program. It focuses on early astronauts John Glenn and Alan Shepard and the growing pains of early space exploration. The movie may be one of the most famous movies about astronauts, but it's not the only one. Here are some other movies that feature on-screen astronauts:

- In *Apollo 13* (1995), three astronauts' lives are at risk when their spacecraft malfunctions. It's a race against time for NASA to save them.
- A crew of astronauts crash-lands on a faraway planet ruled by primates in *Planet of the Apes* (1968, 2001).
- *From the Earth to the Moon* is a 1998 TV miniseries about the Apollo mission to the Moon.
- In *Gravity* (2013), two astronauts, played by Sandra Bullock and George Clooney, must survive in outer space after their spacecraft is destroyed.
- American astronauts and Russian cosmonauts work together on a mission to Jupiter in *2010: The Year We Make Contact* (1984). This movie is a sequel to *2001: A Space Odyssey* (1968).
- Clint Eastwood is a retired astronaut called back to active duty in *Space Cowboys* (2000).

THE CHOSEN FEW

In 1992, the Canadian Space Agency selected its second-ever group of astronauts. Chris Hadfield may be the best known of the bunch. But the other three have also made great contributions to the nation's space program.

Julie Payette has been to space twice (1999, 2009), for a total of 25 days. She was Chief Astronaut for the CSA from 2000 to 2007. She retired from the CSA in 2003.

Dave Williams has also visited space twice (1998, 2007). During his second mission, he performed three spacewalks. He was the third Canadian to walk in space. He remains the record-holder for most spacewalks by a Canadian. He retired from CSA in 2008.

Mike McKay trained as an astronaut for three years, but resigned for medical reasons in 1995. He continued to work as an engineer with CSA, retiring from the program in 1997.

he had originally submitted his application, Chris got the call he had been waiting for. The future he had dreamed of since he had watched Neil Armstrong step on the Moon 23 years earlier had finally come true. Mission accomplished! Chris Hadfield was an astronaut!

Blast Off!

Even though Chris had finally earned his dream job, he didn't get to blast off into space right away. One thing many people don't understand about astronauts, he said, is that they spend very little time in outer space. "I always feel I'm disappointing people when I tell them the truth: we are earthbound, training, most of our working lives."

For Chris, it would be three years of hard work and training before his first mission into orbit. During those years, he focused on technical and safety issues relating to the space

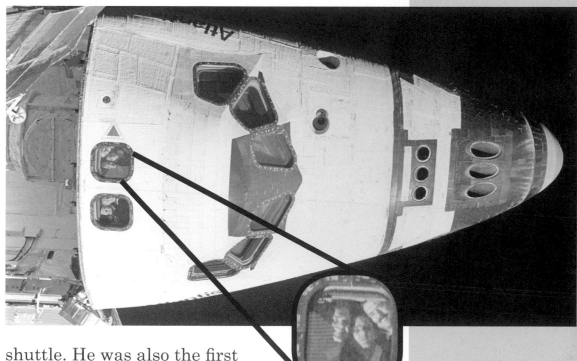

shuttle. He was also the first Canadian to be part of the shuttle launch support team at Kennedy Space Center in Florida. Whenever a shuttle took off into space, Chris was on the ground helping things run smoothly.

His turn to take off finally came on November 12, 1995. That day, he and four U.S. astronauts boarded Space Shuttle *Atlantis* for STS-74, an eight-day mission to Russian space station *Mir*. (STS stands for Space Transportation System. It was the original name of the Space Shuttle Program.)

The ride into orbit took 8 minutes and 42 seconds. "Launch is overwhelming on a sensory level," wrote Chris in 2013. "[You feel] all that speed and all that power, then abruptly, the violence of momentum gives way to the gentle dreaminess of floating on an invisible cushion of air."

November 12, 1995: Five astronauts aboard U.S. Space Shuttle Atlantis *smile for the camera as they look up at the Russian space station* Mir. *The two craft have just met up, and the astronauts will soon board* Mir. *In the detail, Chris Hadfield is easy to spot with his signature mustache!*

Reusable Rockets

NASA's Space Shuttle Program launched on April 12, 1981, with the blast-off of Space Shuttle *Columbia*. Over the next 30 years, space shuttles *Columbia*, *Challenger*, *Discovery*, *Atlantis*, and *Endeavour* took to the skies over and over again. The shuttles used rocket boosters to take off, but glided back to Earth, landing on a runway, much like a passenger jet.

The shuttles transported astronauts into orbit for a total of 135 missions to conduct scientific experiments, repair satellites, and build the International Space Station (ISS).

The program suffered two tragedies. First, in 1986, *Challenger* exploded seconds after liftoff, killing all seven crew members aboard. In February 2003, the program suffered another loss when *Columbia* broke apart at the end of a mission, just before its scheduled landing. Again, seven lives were lost.

In the wake of the *Columbia* accident, then-president George W. Bush announced the Space Shuttle Program would continue, but only until the ISS was completed. NASA would then focus on newer, safer spacecraft.

The Space Shuttle Program ended on July 21, 2011, when *Atlantis* landed, after its final mission, at Kennedy Space Center in Florida. *Atlantis* remains on display there. *Endeavour* is on display in Los Angeles, and *Discovery* is in Virginia.

The main goal of STS-74 was to build a docking module on *Mir*, "so that future Shuttle flights would have a safer, easier way to get on board *Mir* than we did."

During that eight-day mission, Chris became the first Canadian to operate the robotic device called Canadarm in orbit, and the only Canadian ever to board *Mir*.

Years later, an interviewer asked Chris about that first space visit. "Did you ever think a Canadian would fly to space on an American shuttle and visit a Russian space station?" the interviewer asked.

Chris's reply? "No, especially considering I once had a Russian bomber in the gun sights of my F-18 over northern Canada."

SPACE STATION *MIR*

Before the International Space Station (ISS), there was the Soviet (and later Russian) space station *Mir*. Built in seven modules between 1986 and 1996, *Mir* was the world's first long-term research station in orbit, and the world's first spacecraft designed for long-term human occupancy.

The first part of *Mir*, called the core module, was launched in February 1986. Three weeks later, the first two cosmonauts went up to stay. They returned to Earth after 51 days. Another cosmonaut holds the record for longest space visit in history. Dr. Valeri Polyakov lived on *Mir* for 437 days, 17 hours and 38 minutes, beginning in January 1994.

In its 15-year-existence, 104 people from 12 countries visited *Mir*. Chris Hadfield is the only Canadian to have done so.

After ISS was in place, and after orbiting for three times longer than it was expected to, *Mir* was deliberately deorbited. It re-entered Earth's atmosphere, crashing into the South Pacific Ocean, on March 23, 2001.

With a portion of Earth forming a backdrop against the blackness of space, the U.S. Space Shuttle Atlantis *(shown at bottom) pulls away from the Russian space station* Mir. *The photo was taken by Russian cosmonauts piloting a Soyuz spacecraft nearby on July 4, 1995. Later that year, on November 12, Chris Hadfield and four other astronauts were launched to* Mir *aboard* Atlantis *and experienced a procedure similar to the one shown here. The main goal of their eight-day mission: to build a docking module on* Mir *so future astronauts and cosmonauts would have a safer, more convenient portal connecting transport craft to the space station.*

Walking in Space

In 1995, back on Earth after his first trip into orbit, Chris got a job with Mission Control at the Johnson Space Center in Houston, Texas. He became NASA's chief CAPCOM, or capsule communicator, for the Space Shuttle Program. For the next five years and 25 shuttle missions, if an orbiting astronaut ever said, "Houston, we have a problem," it was Chris they were talking to. From an astronaut's perspective, Chris was "Houston."

"The CAPCOM... is constantly analyzing all changing inputs and factors, making countless quick small judgments and decisions, then passing them on to the crew and the ground team," he said. "It's like being coach, quarterback, water boy and cheerleader, all in one."

Chris also represented Canadian astronauts and coordinated their activities as CSA's chief astronaut from 1996 to 2000.

In 2001, Chris got his second shot at spaceflight. Until then, only one other Canadian astronaut—Marc Garneau—had ever made a return visit to space.

On April 19, 2001, Chris and six others blasted off in Space Shuttle *Endeavour* for a 12-day mission to help build the International Space Station (ISS). In addition to Chris, the crew of STS-100 included four Americans, one Italian, and one Russian.

The main goal of this mission was to install Canadarm2 on the ISS. It made sense to have a Canadian on the job for that!

The crews of the ISS and space shuttle Endeavour *are decked out in festive attire for an in-flight, zero-gravity portrait in April 2001. The combined crews included six Americans, two Russians, one Italian, and of course, one Canadian—Chris Hadfield (bottom row, far left).*

Chris Hadfield is shown high above Earth with his feet secured to one Canadian-built robotic arm, called Canadarm, as he works on a new robotic arm, called Canadarm2. Canadarm was attached to the Space Shuttle Endeavour, *and it was used to help connect Canadarm2 to the ISS. The transfer of objects from Canadarm to Canadarm2 was affectionately nicknamed a "Canadian Handshake."*

A HELPING HAND

Canadarm was a robotic arm used to lift, move, hold, and repair objects outside a space shuttle. It was operated from inside the shuttle. Canadarm, which was 49 feet (15 meters) long and could lift more than 66,140 pounds (30,000 kg) on Earth and up to 586,430 pounds (266,000 kg) in space. It was designed and mostly built in Canada, that's why it was called Canadarm.

In total, five Canadarms were built and used by NASA and the CSA between 1981 and 2011. One of those was destroyed when the Space Shuttle *Challenger* exploded just after takeoff in 1986.

By the time Chris Hadfield became the first Canadian to operate Canadarm in orbit in 1995, 42 other astronauts had already used the device. In total, 90 of the 135 space shuttle missions used a Canadarm.

Canadarm was replaced by Canadarm2 in 2011, when the Space Shuttle Program ended. Canadarm2 is attached to the International Space Station.

PHILLIPS ROMINGER ASHBY PARAZYNSKI

6A 100

ЛОНЧАКОВ GUIDONI HADFIELD

Patch for space shuttle mission STS-100.

Canadarm2, "the world's most expensive and sophisticated construction tool," would be used to help complete construction of the ISS over the next 10 years. Chris added to his list of "firsts" on this mission when he became the first Canadian to leave a spacecraft and float freely in space. This is called a spacewalk, and Chris did two of them on this trip, for a total of almost 15 hours outside.

Chris trained for spacewalking in the Neutral Buoyancy Lab, a giant pool at Johnson Space Center in Houston, Texas. He spent about 50 full days practicing in the pool before his first spacewalk.

His first spacewalk didn't go completely smoothly, though. As he was outside tightening bolts on Canadarm2 with a power tool, something inside Chris's helmet made his eyes sting and start to water. Without gravity, the tears didn't fall out of his eyes. Instead, they gathered into a large glob of water, blinding him. "In the space of a few minutes I went from 20/20 vision to blind. In space. Holding a drill."

To his colleagues on the ground, Chris calmly said: "Houston, I have a problem."

As dozens of doctors, engineers, scientists, and other specialists at Mission Control scrambled to figure out what had happened and what to do about it, Chris tried everything he could think of to "unblind" himself. He shook his head and blinked like crazy—and eventually it worked. After about 20 minutes, his eyes stopped stinging, and he started to see again.

It turned out that the problem was a microscopic drop of the fluid used to keep his helmet visor fog-free. That's what got into Chris's eye. NASA now uses a different, less irritating cleaning solution.

> "Being on the ground for six years between my first and second flights made me a much better astronaut and one who had more to contribute both on Earth and off it."
>
> Chris Hadfield

HOME-AWAY-FROM-HOME IN ORBIT

Building the International Space Station (ISS) was truly an international effort. It took scientists, astronauts, cosmonauts, and engineers from 15 different countries 13 years to build what is now the largest structure ever to orbit Earth.

The first module, or segment, of the ISS was launched in November 1998. It was another two years before enough of it was built that people could live there. On November 2, 2000, one American astronaut and two Russian cosmonauts became the first to arrive and live on the ISS. The space station has been continually occupied ever since.

Up to ten people live on the ISS at any given time. Most stay for four to six months.

The ISS has three research laboratories, six sleeping compartments (each the size of a phone booth), two bathrooms, a gym, and more living space than a typical six-bedroom house. It is almost four times the size of Russian space station *Mir*.

"The ISS is a one million-pound (455,000-kg) spaceship that's the size of a football field, including end zones," said Chris. "It's so big, with so many discrete modules, that it's possible to go nearly a full day without seeing another crewmate."

It's so big, in fact, that you can see it from Earth with your naked eye. NASA has a website that tells you when to look up to see it: **http://spotthestation.nasa.gov/**. It also has its own Facebook page.

Scenes from outside and inside the International Space Station. Top: The ISS as viewed from a departing space shuttle. Bottom: Inside the ISS, the two sets of crew members for Expedition 35 settle into their places after the docking of a Soyuz capsule with the ISS. Expedition 35 Commander Chris Hadfield (center) welcomes newly arrived Russian cosmonauts Alexander Misurkin (left) and Pavel Vinogradov (right).

Assignment: Earth

Soon after his second spaceflight, Chris became NASA's Director of Operations at the Yuri Gagarin Cosmonaut Training Center in Star City, Russia. (Star City is located about an hour from Moscow—Russia's capital city.)

His job was to direct ISS crew activities in Russia. He also oversaw support staff training and negotiated with Russian and other international space programs as needed.

While he was in Star City, Chris learned as much as he could about Russian space technology and equipment. He trained to fly the Soyuz spacecraft, and to perform spacewalks in Russian spacesuits, which are different from

> *"Spacewalking is like rock climbing, weightlifting, repairing a small engine and performing an intricate pas de deux—simultaneously, while encased in a bulky suit that's scraping your knuckles, fingertips and collarbone raw. In zero gravity, many easy tasks become incredibly difficult. Just turning a wrench to loosen a bolt can be like trying to change a tire while wearing ice skates and goalie mitts."*
>
> Chris Hadfield, *An Astronaut's Guide to Life on Earth*

NASA's spacesuits. He learned about being a cosmonaut versus an astronaut. He qualified as a flight engineer in the Russian system.

He also plunged himself into Russian life, learning about the culture and people. He learned to speak Russian. He ate, drank, and danced with his Russian neighbors.

In 2003, Colonel Chris Hadfield left his position in Russia when he retired from the Royal Canadian Air Force after 25 years of duty.

For the next seven years, as a civilian astronaut, Chris held a variety of earthbound jobs. He was chief of robotics for the NASA Astronaut Office in Houston before being named Chief of International Space Station Operations in 2006. He later served as commander for an underwater project called NEEMO (NASA Extreme Environment Mission Operations), designed to simulate space experiences.

As if that wasn't enough, though, Chris Hadfield's greatest assignment was yet to come.

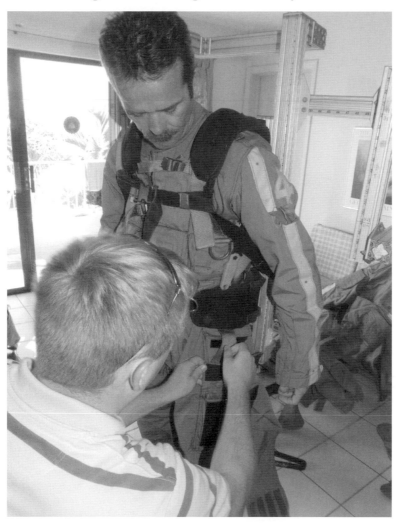

In May 2010, Chris Hadfield prepares for a check of the gear he will wear as commander of NEEMO 14, a two-week training mission on the ocean floor. One purpose of the mission is to prepare astronauts for spacewalks and other EVA (extravehicular activity) outside the International Space Station.

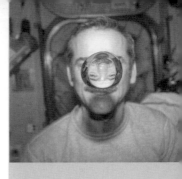

Chapter 5
The Last Blast

In late fall 2009, NASA assigned Chris Hadfield the greatest mission of his career. He was to become commander of the International Space Station (ISS)—the first Canadian ever to hold the lofty position. "It was something I'd been working toward my whole adult life," said Chris. "I was both proud to get the assignment and humbled by it." He had three years to prepare for the top job in outer space.

All Systems (Not Quite) Go

Chris Hadfield knew that his third trip to space would likely be his final visit, and his "last chance to make a real contribution to the space program." He wanted to make the most of it, and to make sure he was "worthy of the honor" that NASA and CSA had given him.

December 19, 2012: Wearing fake mustaches and peering out of cardboard "spaceships," friends and relatives show their support for Chris near the site of his final launch to the ISS from Baikonur, Kazakhstan.

LONGEST-DISTANCE RELATIONSHIP

Many couples have long-distance relationships. But Chris and Helene Hadfield may be able to claim the longest-distance relationship of all. For five months in 2012–2013, they didn't even live on the same planet!

Spending time away from her husband is nothing new for Helene. Because of Chris's work, they have lived much of their 30-plus-years of marriage apart.

They managed to make it work, though, partly because Helene decided early on to let her husband be the superstar in the family. She realized that he had one shot at his dream, and the only way he could achieve it was with her support. "We worked hard together to make that happen," she said.

As the spouse of an astronaut, Helene has uprooted her family over and over again because of her husband's postings around the world. She has coped with the fame that follows Chris wherever he goes. She has also coped with other women following Chris wherever he goes.

The upside is that she has traveled the world with her husband. Together, the couple has visited more than 50 countries around the globe. Helene has worked at many different jobs and experienced a wide range of cultures. She speaks Russian. "I love variety, and that's what has made this life so great," she said.

Now that Chris has retired from astronaut-hood, he and Helene have settled in Toronto. Chris is the first to acknowledge that he wouldn't be where he is without Helene. With these words, he dedicated his book, *An Astronaut's Guide to Life on Earth*, to her: "Your confidence, impetus and endless help made these dreams come true."

Chris and Helene Hadfield are shown in 2014 learning about the sport of hurling on a visit to Ireland, where their daughter Kristin lives.

For the next two years, he worked hard—and spent hundreds of extra hours in training—to become a specialist in almost every system on the ISS. He wanted to make sure that, as commander of ISS Expedition 35, he was ready to "operate, understand and repair" just about anything on board.

What he didn't count on was that his body might not be space-ready.

In October 2011, just 14 months before his scheduled liftoff, Chris felt a pain in his stomach. Over the next few days, he became sicker and sicker, until doctors decided he needed a small operation.

They discovered "a glob of sticky scar tissue" in his abdomen, fixed it up, and sent him home. This wasn't the first time Chris had experienced this, though. The problem stemmed from a childhood operation that had left scar tissue in his stomach. In 1990, Chris had surgery to deal with it, but after this second flare-up, Chris knew it had now become a medical issue that could ground him. "If there was any chance of getting so ill that I'd need to be evacuated from the ISS, I had a responsibility to withdraw from the expedition," he said.

For the next five months, Chris continued to train "to get ready for an expedition I might or might not lead." At the same time, a team of medical experts consulted, studied, and worked to determine whether he was healthy enough to go into orbit. The committee had to be convinced there was no danger that Chris would become ill in space.

That wasn't the only concern, though. If Chris were to withdraw as commander of Expedition

35, a whole series of future missions would also be affected. Because of his particular set of skills, there was no backup for him within CSA or NASA—and no way to get anyone safely trained in time. If he was pulled from the mission, it could be disastrous to the entire space program.

Chris believed he was space-ready, so he set out to prove it to the medical committee.

For five months, he researched, talked to experts, studied risk factors, and collected data,

THE CALM BEFORE THE LAUNCH

For up to two weeks before launch, astronauts are quarantined, or isolated, from the rest of the world. That's to make sure they don't catch a bug that could make them sick in space. It's also to give them time to "pause, consider what they are about to do and begin to transition to a new kind of existence," said Chris, who was quarantined for 12 days in Kazakhstan before his final mission.

During this forced "time-out," astronauts' and cosmonauts' every need is looked after. They get to relax, reflect, exercise, unwind in the sauna, pack their personal items, and dine on excellent food in a stress-free environment.

Still, quarantine can be hard on them. They are about to leave the planet for many months, and they are only allowed brief, arm's-length (or behind-glass) visits from family members—who have practically been sterilized to make sure they don't bring any illnesses with them. The flight crew members spend their last days on Earth largely separated from their loved ones.

On December 13, 2012, six days before his December 19 launch to the ISS, Chris Hadfield plays a game of pool while under quarantine.

but the medical team still wasn't convinced Chris was safe to fly.

Finally, one committee member suggested that Chris go for an ultrasound. This is a type of screening test that uses sound waves to view and create images of your insides from the outside of your body. This test would be the deciding factor in Chris's future as an astronaut.

If he failed the test, Chris would be grounded. He would spend the rest of his life as "the commander-who-wasn't." After all his hard work and preparation, a health issue beyond his control could end his career as an astronaut. "After years of studying and training, this was what it all came down to," he said.

In March 2012, nine months before he was scheduled to blast off for his final NASA mission, Chris arrived at the hospital for his ultrasound. A doctor slid a sort of sensor over Chris's skin to peer inside his abdomen. After a few tense minutes, the doctor smiled. The test proved Chris was OK to fly.

Before Chris embarked on ISS Expedition 34/35 in December 2012, he and his two crewmates served as the backup crew for an earlier mission, Expedition 32/33. From right, Chris and his two backup crewmates, Roman Romanenko and Tom Marshburn, pose from behind glass while under quarantine with the prime crew members, from far left, Akihiko Hoshide, Yuri Malenchenko, and Sunita Williams.

SLIGHTLY SUPERSTITIOUS

Astronauts and cosmonauts are scientists—but that doesn't prevent them from performing a few good-luck rituals before space flights. Here are a few practiced in Baikonur, Kazakhstan:

- Everyone who has blasted off from Baikonur since the 1970s has watched the popular Russian film *White Sun of the Desert* in the days before launch.
- They also pee on the back, right tire of the bus that takes them to the launch pad. Rumor has it that the first cosmonaut, Yuri Gagarin, did this, so now they all do.
- They sign the door of the bedroom they stayed in during quarantine.
- It is considered bad luck for the crew to view the rocket before launch day. So instead of getting to see the rocket being rolled out onto the launch pad before the day of the launch, they are kept busy getting haircuts on that day.
- They listen to certain music at certain times leading up to launch.
- They take a stuffed toy in the Russian Soyuz capsule with them. It dangles from a chain in view of a video camera. The toy serves as a mascot, but when it starts to float, it also signals to the ground crew that the spacecraft has reached orbit.

Chris Hadfield performs the ritual of signing the door to the room he stayed in during quarantine prior to leaving the Cosmonaut Hotel in Baikonur, Kazakhstan, for the launch of ISS Expedition 34/35.

OLD RELIABLE

First used in the 1960s, the Russian-built Soyuz spacecraft is the most common, safest, most reliable, and most cost-efficient launch system in the world. Because it works so well, it hasn't changed much in its 50-year history. "Just because it's simpler doesn't mean it's worse," than the space shuttle, said Chris Hadfield, one of the few NASA and CSA astronauts trained on Soyuz. "Sometimes if it's good enough, then [it's best to] just build another one." No need to fix what isn't broke, as the saying goes.

On December 12, 2012, a Soyuz spacecraft (wrapped in black) is fitted into its booster rocket near the launch site in Baikonur, Kazakhstan. This is the ship that carried Chris Hadfield and his crewmates to the ISS on December 19.

A Soyuz spacecraft as viewed from the International Space Station against a backdrop of clouds in Earth's atmosphere below.

The future Commander Hadfield breathed a huge sigh of relief. "But there wasn't time to celebrate," he said. "I had work to do. I was going to space, after all."

New Kids on the Block

On December 19, 2012, Chris Hadfield, along with U.S. astronaut Tom Marshburn and Russian cosmonaut Roman Romanenko, blasted off from Baikonur, Kazakhstan.

Before launch, Chris vowed to himself that he would "make the most of every moment of this

From top to bottom in white spacesuits: Chris Hadfield, U.S. astronaut Tom Marshburn, and Russian cosmonaut Roman Romanenko wave as they board a Soyuz rocket for their launch to the ISS.

SCIENCE IN THE SKY

The main function of the ISS is to serve as a research lab in space. Every crew that lives there performs experiments. Chris Hadfield and his crewmates on Expedition 34/35 worked on more than 130 experiments during their time on the ISS. About half were related to learning more about the effects living in space has on the human body. They also studied such things as the impact space travel has on spacecraft, what the universe is made of, and how different types of particles behave under different conditions.

Chris Hadfield at work in a laboratory aboard the ISS in January 2013.

incredible journey, to engrave its details on my memory."

Unlike his previous blast into outer space, this one didn't begin in the space shuttle. The Space Shuttle Program had ended a year earlier. This time, Chris and his colleagues left Earth in the much smaller, much simpler Russian Soyuz spacecraft.

Upon their arrival on the ISS, this trio of flight engineers joined Expedition 34, already in progress. By that point, Commander Kevin Ford and two cosmonauts had already been living and working on the space station for two months. An overlap period with these experienced crew members gave Chris, Tom, and Roman time to learn the ropes before they moved up the ranks.

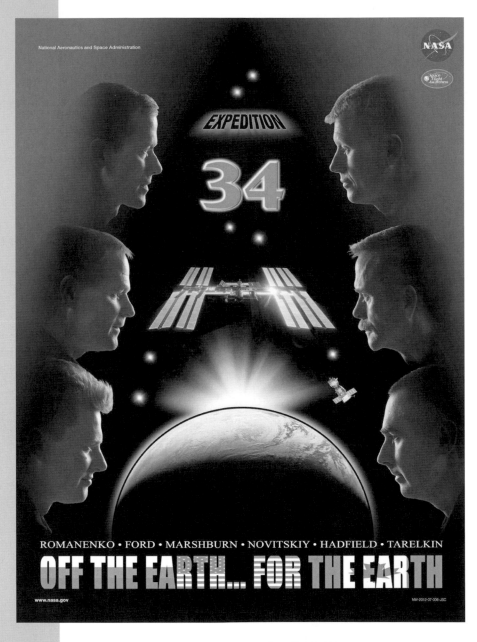

The official NASA poster for ISS Expedition 34. The poster includes a dramatic depiction of the Sun "rising" over Earth, illuminating the faces of the mission's three soon-to-be former crew members and three newcomers, including Chris Hadfield (right, second from top).

Playing Well with Others

When astronauts spend several months together in close quarters on the ISS, it helps if they get along well. Chris said he has heard rumors of tensions rising so high during early space missions that crew members came to blows, or they refused to speak to each other for days on end. "So these days," he said, "NASA looks for a certain type of person, someone who plays well with others."

On his final mission, Chris was very happy with his assigned crewmates. Tom Marshburn and Roman Romanenko "are two of the most easygoing and pleasant people on or off the planet," he said. They were also highly technically skilled, and had excellent work ethics.

Chris earned equally high praise from his colleagues. "If you're going to be cooped up in a can—a can with a beautiful view—for six months, Chris is the guy you want to be with," said Tom.

"I count myself really lucky [because] I don't have to show up there and be in charge," said Chris before his arrival on the ISS. "Eventually I'm going to be asked to command the space station, but I don't have to jump in and be full speed running and take over right away. I can do a bunch of on-the-job training."

The new crew members also needed time to adjust to living in their new, out-of-this world home.

Astro-Fact

The walls in some rooms in the ISS are almost completely covered with Velcro. Without gravity, things just float around. They can drift away, never to be seen again. Or they might turn up in the wrong place, risking damage to equipment or people. To make sure things stay put, astronauts stick them to the walls, ceiling, and floors of the space station.

It's normal for astronauts to feel like throwing up when they first arrive in space. The human body is confused by weightlessness. It can't figure out which way is up, and which is down, without gravity there to tell it.

At first, "you're disoriented and clumsy," said Chris. "It's like being a baby bird and not quite knowing how to fly yet." Newly arrived crew members risk crashing into things while they float around. On occasion, newbies struggling to get their bearings have accidentally bumped into scientific experiments, destroying months or years of research.

One of the first things Chris and his crewmates had to do when they arrived on the ISS was pose for a cramped photo op. Then they conducted a live, televised press conference. Everyone in Mission Control could see the astronauts, but the astronauts couldn't see them—they could only hear their voices. "[It] was also our first chance to speak to our families since launch," said Chris. "[It was] a public private event, complete with reporters."

Next up for the new guys were a safety briefing and a tour of the ISS, followed by days of adjusting to a new way of life—a different time zone, the noise on the ISS, the sleeping arrangements, lack of privacy, lack of running water, slurping food out of pouches, and floating instead of walking.

Going Where No Canadian Has Gone Before

After three months on the space station, Chris and his colleagues were ready for their new ISS

National Aeronautics and Space Administration

THE EXPEDITION

CASSIDY • ROMANENKO • HADFIELD • VINOGRADOV • MISURKIN • MARSHBURN

www.nasa.gov

The official NASA crew poster for ISS Expedition 35. In addition to Commander Chris Hadfield (third from left) and his "old" Expedition 34 mates Roman Romanenko (second from left) and Tom Marshburn (far right), the crew included newcomers Chris Cassidy (far left), Pavel Vinogradov (third from right), and Alexander Misurkin (second from right).

roles. On March 14, 2013, with an on-board ceremony and a salute, Chris became ISS Commander Chris Hadfield. "It's a huge honor and a privilege for me ... but also [for] all my co-workers at the Canadian Space Agency and my entire country," said Chris during the ceremony.

The following day, outgoing Commander Kevin Ford and his crew departed from the ISS. Two weeks later, on March 28, three new crew members, including future ISS Commander Pavel Vinogradov, arrived to join Expedition 35. Chris, Tom, and Roman were no longer the new kids on the block!

As space station commander, Chris was in charge of all the science, systems, and people aboard the ISS. He made sure team members worked well—together and as individuals. He was responsible for the crew's safety and well-being. He was chief troubleshooter, problemsolver, and moralebooster.

Because of his extensive training, Chris was also prepared to address any technical or mechanical problem that occurred on the ISS under his watch. In short, Chris was captain of the ship from March 14 to May 12, 2013, the day he handed over command to the next leader.

By the time he left the ISS on May 13, though, Chris was no longer just an ordinary astronaut. By then, magazines and online media

"To be able to command the space station, yes, is professional, and yes, I'll take it seriously, and yes, it's important to Canada, but for me, as just a Canadian kid, it makes me want to shout and laugh and do cartwheels."

Chris Hadfield, shortly before launch

ISS Info

- The ISS circles Earth every 92 minutes, meaning astronauts on board experience 16 sunrises and 16 sunsets every day.
- It flies at almost 5 miles per second (8 km/s). That's fast enough to go to the Moon and back in about a day.
- The ISS orbits Earth at an altitude of 200 to 270 miles (322 to 435 km).
- Sixteen countries were involved in building the ISS.
- At a cost of more than $120 billion, the ISS is the most expensive object ever built.
- The ISS is the third-brightest object in the night sky after the Moon and Venus.

High above New Zealand, spacewalking NASA and European Space Agency (ESA) astronauts assemble a portion of the ISS.

were calling him "the most famous spaceman since Neil Armstrong," "the most famous astronaut on Earth," and "the most famous and beloved astronaut since Apollo 11 and certainly the best-known Canadian astronaut ever."

Why did he reach such superstar status? It wasn't because Chris was a better commander than any of the previous ISS commanders. It was because, while he orbited our planet, this down-to-Earth former farm boy generously, and continually, shared his out-of-this-world experiences with millions of ordinary Earthlings.

Chapter 6
Commander Cool

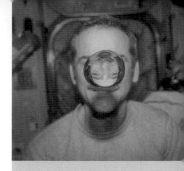

Chris Hadfield loves being in space. He loves gazing at the "kaleidoscopic... glory" of Earth from above. He loves the scientific advancement, and the daily discoveries that flight crews make on the International Space Station (ISS). He knows, though, that visiting outer space is a rare honor that most of us will never experience. So on this last trip, Chris made it his mission to bring everyone on Earth along for the ride.

@Cmdr_Hadfield

Before his launch from Baikonur, Kazakhstan, on December 19, 2012, Chris had a Twitter account with about 20,000 followers. He also loved taking photographs—the beauty of planet Earth was one of his favorite subjects. Before he took off, his son Evan urged him to combine these two things while he was living on the ISS.

At the time, Evan was a 27-year-old marketing specialist who understood the power of social media. He suggested that his father "stop *telling* people how inspiring the space program is, and start *showing* them."

Below: A photo of a storm system on Earth sent from space via Twitter by Chris Hadfield aboard the International Space Station, with the following caption: "Tonight's Finale: When I look at thunderstorms from above, I see faces. What do you see in the clouds?"

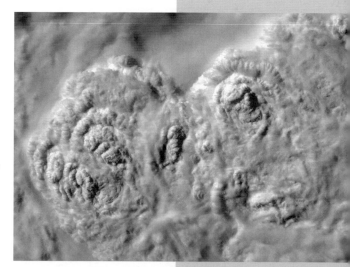

On December 21, Chris tweeted his first photos from the space station. His very first tweet was a photo of himself, floating in space with a huge smile on his face.

Two days later, he recorded a song, which Evan uploaded to SoundCloud. The song, "Jewel in the Night," was written by Chris's brother Dave, and it was the first song ever recorded on the ISS. Chris tweeted a link to the recording so his followers could listen to it.

That song got Evan thinking about *all* the sounds in space and the noises on the ISS that most people will never hear in person. He encouraged his dad to record those, too. Father obliged, and son posted the recordings on SoundCloud, reposting them to Twitter.

A photo taken on Christmas Day, 2012, aboard the ISS.

"I decided that I was not going to try and keep the experience of flying into space for myself. I wanted to use whatever I could to share my experiences with the world. Just prior to my stay on the ISS, NASA finally figured out how to get regular, limited Internet access on the station. So I thought that it would be a great way to invite everyone on board with us."

Chris Hadfield, 2014

By then, Chris was also shooting short vidcos about the "only-in-space aspects of everyday life," such as how to clean up a spill in space, how to cut your hair in space, and how to exercise in zero gravity. "Thanks to the Internet, we could *show* people what it's like to be in space, in real time," said Chris.

The CSA posted these videos to its website and on YouTube—and viewers couldn't get enough of them. In total, Chris made 146 videos in English and French during his five-month spaceflight.

Chris's earthbound fans' response to the sights and sounds of space was instantaneous and international. Within three weeks, he had 115,000 Twitter followers from around the world, and stories about the online astronaut began appearing in the international news media. Evan became his father's social media manager, spending up to 16 hours a day posting and reposting to various accounts.

By the time Chris returned to Earth five months later, he had about 900,000 Twitter

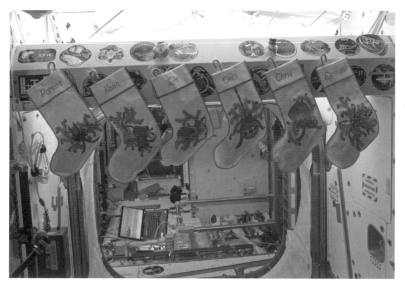

Chris's stocking, along with those of fellow members of ISS Expedition 34, was hung with care on December 25, 2012, in an area that connects the U.S. and Russian segments of the International Space Station.

This photo, taken under the watch of Expedition 35 Commander Chris Hadfield from the ISS in April 2013, shows a bank of clouds in the Pacific Ocean off the coast of Southern California and the Baja California Peninsula in Mexico. The recessed area to the left is the Los Angeles Basin, a geological formation that includes portions of the Los Angeles metropolitan area.

science experiments with schoolchildren via video link. He contacted students in remote Canadian communities through amateur radio. He held press conferences in space. He sang a song called "I.S.S. (Is Somebody Singing?)" live from the space station, accompanied by a group of high school students in Toronto, and Ed Robertson, the lead singer of Canadian band Barenaked Ladies.

In mid-February 2013, Chris took part in an "epic" Ask Me Anything session on Reddit that drew 7,786 comments and questions. He also participated in NASA's first-ever live-from-space Google+ Hangout.

"He's very social, and one of the best things about this mission is that people can see Chris's quirky sense of humor. He's not afraid to kind of be out there, showing his enjoyment. And he's a workaholic, but he doesn't think of it that way—it's all fun."

Helene Hadfield, 2013

Then there was the moment when, in the words of a cyberbuzz.com blogger, "[people on] the Internet lost their collective minds." That day, February 3, Chris tweeted back-and-forth with the original—fictional—starship commander, Capt. James T. Kirk, aka actor William Shatner of *Star Trek*. "A real space captain, tweeted a fake space captain, and the world was perfect," the blogger wrote. Here's how the tweet went:

Shatner:
"@Cmdr_Hadfield Are you
tweeting from space?"

Hadfield:
"@WilliamShatner Yes, Standard
Orbit, Captain. And we're detecting
signs of life on the surface."

Chris's greatest social media moment came just days before he left orbit and returned to Earth. On May 12, 2013, he posted a made-on-the-ISS video of himself performing David Bowie's 1969 song "Space Oddity." Within days, seven million viewers had watched it. (The number of YouTube views has since risen to more than 26 million.) David Bowie called it "possibly the most poignant version of the song ever created."

Because of copyright rules, the video was removed from YouTube after one year. Six months later, though, after negotiations with David Bowie's people, Chris had permission to put the video back online. It will be on YouTube until at least November 2016.

Chris Hadfield joins a concert held in Houston while aboard the ISS in February 2013. Members of the Irish musical group The Chieftains joined the Houston Symphony Orchestra and other musicians, including two other astronauts. Chris appears on the video screen above.

magazine *Quartz*. "Perhaps what made Hadfield such a hit may have less to do with the mere fact that he was tweeting from space—plenty of other astronauts have done the same— but that he talked about sports and his kids and he made stupid jokes. A lot of people use social media for such ordinary things. That he was doing it from space is what made it extraordinary."

Unfortunately, all good things must come to an end. On May 12, 2013, with his just-released "Space Oddity" music video earning thousands of views by the minute, Chris handed over command of the ISS to cosmonaut Pavel Vinogradov. The following day, he and his Expedition 35 crewmates, Tom Marshburn and

Roman Romanenko, bid farewell to the ISS.

Before his departure, Chris sent a final tweet from the space station—a photo, completely black except for a curve of blue-and-orange light, with the words, "Spaceflight finale: To some this may look like a sunset. But it's a new dawn."

The world's favorite astronaut was coming down to Earth.

"I'm sorry ... but ... could you be any cooler?"

Facebook comment from a fan

On the day before Chris Hadfield (upper right) and other Expedition 35 crewmates returned to Earth, he turned over command of the ISS to the commander of Expedition 36, cosmonaut Pavel Vinogradov (upper left). In this photo, members of both expeditions take part in an ISS ritual—placing expedition logo decals in various locations on the ISS.

Chapter 7
Down to Earth

On May 14, 2013, its landing cushioned by parachutes and guided by a system of engines, the Soyuz capsule carrying Chris Hadfield, Tom Marshburn, and Roman Romanenko struck Earth on the steppes, or grasslands, of Kazakhstan. The spacecraft rolled over a few times before coming to a stop. "I [was] upside down, hanging heavily in my straps from the ceiling, stunned, shaken, stirred," remembered Chris. Gravity had done its duty. After traveling 62 million miles (100 million km), completing 2,336 Earth orbits, and living in space for 146 days, @Cmdr_Hadfield was home.

Below: Crammed into quarters aboard their Soyuz capsule, Expedition 35 members Tom Marshburn, Roman Romanenko, and Chris Hadfield prepare to undock from the ISS and return to Earth after about five months in space.

With its parachute trailing behind, the Soyuz capsule carrying ISS Expedition 35 crew members Hadfield, Romanenko, and Marshburn hits a remote area of Kazakhstan upon its return to Earth.

Re-entry

Immediately after landing, Chris, who had been called "the coolest man on (and off) Earth," didn't look so cool. Five months in space takes a toll on the human body, and suddenly moving from a weightless world to one with gravity was crippling for him and the other crew members.

Chris, Tom, and Roman had to be lifted out of the Soyuz capsule and carried to waiting chairs. Having been in a sunless environment for months, the morning light was blinding for them. Space agency officials, politicians, photographers, and medical personnel crowded

From left, Expedition 35 Commander Hadfield and ISS crewmates Romanenko and Marshburn are placed in chairs and treated to medical attention, phone calls, and photo ops after being removed from the Soyuz capsule.

SPACE TRAVEL TIDBITS

- First person in space: Cosmonaut Yuri Gagarin, April 12, 1961.
    - First animals in space: fruit flies, February 20, 1947; followed by a monkey named Albert II, June 14, 1949.
- Total number of humans who have been to space (as of April 2015): 541.
- Total time humans have spent in space (adding up all missions): 124 years.
- Longest single stay in space: Cosmonaut Valeri Polyakov; beginning January 8, 1994, spent 437 days, 17 hours, and 38 minutes in space.
- Most time in space for a single traveler: Cosmonaut Sergei Krikalev; in six missions, between 1988 and 2005, spent a total of 803 days, 9 hours, and 39 minutes in space.
- Most trips to space: Two U.S. astronauts have visited space seven times each. Jerry Ross made his first trip in November 1985, with his final visit in April 2002. Franklin Chang-Díaz made his first visit in January 1986, with his final trip in June 2002.
- First person to spacewalk: Cosmonaut Alexei Leonov stepped outside a spacecraft for about 12 minutes on March 18, 1965.
- Most spacewalks in a career: Cosmonaut Anatoly Solovyev took 16 spacewalks between 1990 and 1998.
- Longest individual spacewalks: On March 11, 2001, astronauts Susan Helms and Jim Voss spent 8 hours and 56 minutes outside the ISS.

Longest stay in space: Valeri Polyakov.

Most time in space: Sergei Krikalev.

Longest individual spacewalks: Susan Helms and Jim Voss (shown with Chris Hadfield, left).

Most trips to space: Jerry Ross (top) and Franklin Chang-Díaz.

Still feeling unsteady after returning from months in space, Expedition 34/35 crewmates (from left) Tom Marshburn, Roman Romanenko, and Chris Hadfield are honored at a welcoming ceremony at the Karaganda Airport in Kazakhstan on May 14, 2013. In addition to being presented with traditional Kazakh clothing, the crew received Russian "nesting" dolls bearing their likenesses (below).

around the flight crew, "overwhelming" them after the quiet of space.

As soon as his helmet came off, the first thing Chris did was talk to Helene via satellite phone. Photographers recorded the moment.

Fifteen minutes later, Chris and his crewmates were carried to a medical tent. After a quick cleanup, checkup, and some medical attention, attendants carried them to an armored truck, which delivered them to a waiting helicopter.

An hour later, they arrived in Karaganda, the nearest city to their remote landing location, for a welcome ceremony and press conference. The first question for Chris was, "Did you know that 'Space Oddity' has had seven million hits?" He didn't know, and he was feeling so sick at that moment, he could barely answer the question.

Next stop for Chris was Houston, Texas, where Helene was waiting for him. At one of the stopovers along the way, he took his first

> *"Safely home—back on Earth, happily readapting to the heavy pull of gravity. Wonderful to smell and feel Spring."*
>
> Chris Hadfield's first message to his Twitter followers upon landing

shower in five months. Of course, he tweeted about that to his Twitter followers!

After the 20-hour journey, husband and wife were finally reunited on U.S. soil. Still, the exhausted astronaut wasn't allowed to go home. Medical personnel had work to do. They put Chris through two and a half hours of tests, examining everything from his hand-eye coordination to balance and blood pressure.

Finally, Chris was allowed to sleep. "I don't think I've ever been as happy to go to bed as I was that night," he said. "After months of being able to somersault effortlessly through the air, I could barely hold my head up."

A few days later, Chris was still "tottering around like an old man." He had to relearn how to live in a gravity-based body. He even had to learn how to talk properly again, because his tongue, which had adjusted to zero gravity, now weighed heavily in his mouth.

"It's very confusing for my body now," said Chris at the time. "My body was quite happy in space without gravity."

He felt sick to his stomach and dizzy much of the time. It hurt his tailbone to sit down. It hurt his back and his feet to stand up.

He lost his balance and bumped into

ASTRO-FACT

Chris's first post-ISS meal included a sandwich, raw vegetables, and fruit.

things. He was exhausted.

For six weeks, Chris endured a stream of post-space medical tests—partly to make sure he was healthy, partly so that scientists could learn more about the effects space has on the human body.

In zero gravity, the blood, heart, and circulation change. Bones lose calcium and become more brittle. Muscles get weaker. These are some of the same things that happen to the human body as it ages. By studying Chris's post-space body, scientists were able to learn more about the aging process. "For the first few months back, astronauts are essentially outsized lab rats," said Chris.

What Now, Earthling?

In addition to hours and hours of physical rehabilitation, Chris's first few weeks post-landing were filled with press conferences, public appearances, meetings, and debriefings about the mission.

What fans of the "pop astronaut" didn't know at this point, though, was that their favorite spaceman was about to retire. He had announced this quietly to the CSA and NASA months earlier.

In June, Chris traveled with fellow astronaut Tom Marshburn back to Russia. There, they were reunited with their ISS crewmate Roman Romanenko for the official Russian welcome-back-to-Earth celebrations

ASTRO-FACT

Because Chris's body was so confused and clumsy after living in space, it was three weeks after his return before doctors cleared him to drive a car, and two months before he was allowed to go for a run outside on his own.

and debrief. For Chris, "it was the last leg of a 21-year career as an astronaut."

He knew this would be his last time working with friends and colleagues at Star City—and he admitted to feeling "melancholy" about closing this particular chapter in his life. At the same time, though, he looked forward to finding out what new adventures life had in store for him and Helene.

A week later, back in Canada, on June 10, 2013, Chris Hadfield publically announced his pending retirement from the Canadian Space Agency. On Twitter that day, he posted a photo of his CSA colleagues applauding him, with the words: "To say goodbye to these good people today was much harder than I expected."

On July 1, at the invitation of Canada's prime minister, Chris took part in Canada Day celebrations on Parliament Hill in Ottawa. Throngs of cheering fans came to hear their high-flying hero sing "Space Oddity" and "Is Somebody Singing?" in the nation's capital.

It was Chris's last public gig as a CSA/NASA astronaut. Three days later, Chris was officially a retired person.

He spent his first day off the job in Calgary, Alberta, preparing for his role as parade marshal for the world-famous Calgary Stampede Parade. Organizers had invited Chris to serve in the cowboy-themed position of honor—via Twitter, of course—while he was still orbiting the planet.

At a press conference that day, Chris showed off his new, made-to-order cowboy boots—complete with ISS expedition patch inlaid on the front, and a maple leaf on the back. "Today,"

Chris Hadfield gives the thumbs-up sign following a Canada Day celebration rehearsal on June 30, 2013, in Ottawa.

SPACE TOURISM

These days, you don't necessarily have to be an astronaut to visit the International Space Station. Pretty much anybody can go—anyone with a spare $50 million, that is.

Between 2001 and 2009, seven space tourists have vacationed on the ISS. Each trip has lasted from 8 to 15 days. All have blasted off from Earth in Soyuz spacecraft, courtesy of the Russian Federal Space Agency.

One fellow liked it so much, he went twice, for a total of 29 days. The combined fare for his 2007 and 2009 adventures was about $60 million.

In 2010, Russia called a temporary halt to these "personal spaceflights." With the Space Shuttle Program winding down in 2011, space agencies needed every seat in the small Soyuz craft to send actual astronauts to the ISS.

The Russian Federal Space Agency has since announced it is once again open for tourists. In 2012, popular British singer Sarah Brightman announced her plans to become the next civilian to fly to the ISS. In May 2015, after several months of preflight training, she withdrew from the flight, which was scheduled for September 2015, citing "personal family reasons." When her backup, a Japanese business person, also withdrew from the flight, the Russian agency announced that Kazakh cosmonaut Aidyn Aimbetov had been added to the flight.

British soprano Sarah Brightman is shown at the Yuri Gagarin Cosmonaut Training Center in Star City, Russia, in March 2015, where she was on hand to wish members of the Expedition 43 crew good luck prior to their launch for the ISS. In May, she would announce her withdrawal from her scheduled trip to the ISS.

he said, "is a brave new day." Like the first time he walked in space, Chris was once again stepping into unknown territory.

Since that first day of retired life, though, the former fighter pilot/test pilot/astronaut hasn't exactly put his feet up. In fact, he's barely taken a break.

Chris has become a highly sought-after consultant and public speaker, participating in many events every year. He has been interviewed for books, newspapers, magazines, radio, television, and talk shows.

Five months after his Soyuz capsule landed on the plains of Kazakhstan, Chris's first book, *An Astronaut's Guide to Life on Earth*, came out. An instant

Chris joins his daughter Kristin in Dublin, Ireland, for a guest appearance on a popular Irish TV program, The Late Late Show.

The Canadian Embassy in London, England, is "guarded" by two figures in spacesuits on the night of an appearance by Chris Hadfield. His visit to London was part of a tour to promote the publication of his first book, An Astronaut's Guide to Life on Earth.

Late-Night Funny Guy

Back on Earth, Chris's engaging personality, quick wit, and treasure trove of stories and pictures of his time in space, have made him a huge hit on talk shows. In an interview with late-night host Conan O'Brien, Chris described how astronauts packed their dirty laundry into "a little unmanned resupply ship," ejected it into space, and allowed it to burn up during re-entry into Earth's atmosphere!

Conan O'Brien:
*"Wait a minute! You're kidding…. You guys
in the space station are throwing your
underwear out—your dirty underwear—
out the window,
and it's raining down on us?"*

Chris Hadfield:
*"So you know how, when you're sitting in a
corner of a room, and there's that really sharp
sunbeam coming across, and you can see
those lovely little motes of dust that are
falling down, delicately through
the sunbeam?... Yeah. That's my underwear."*

international bestseller, it became the basis for a TV sitcom being developed by ABC, with Chris as one of the show's producers.

His second book came out a year later. It is called *You Are Here: Around the World in 92 Minutes*, and it is a collection of photos of places around the globe that Chris took aboard the ISS.

In March 2014, in Vancouver, British Columbia, Chris presented a TED Talk called "What I Learned from Going Blind in Space." A vivid set of descriptions and impressions based

Chris Hadfield is interviewed at the Royal Geographic Society in London in December 2014 following the publication of his second book, You Are Here: Around the World in 92 Minutes. *Shown here is one of the many photographs that Chris took while aboard the ISS.*

Shining Star

Chris knows that, in the rapid-fire Internet world we inhabit, it's likely that his moment in the Sun will fade before long. "The blast of glory that attends launch and landing doesn't last long. The spotlight moves on, and astronauts need to, too."

In the meantime, while he is famous around the world, he has become "infamous" within NASA. "He has put pressure on everybody," laughed the head of the space agency in the fall of 2014. "Chris has revolutionized the way that

Students in Pearland, Texas, line up to speak with members of Expedition 35, under the command of Chris Hadfield, via a live feed from the ISS in April 2013. Chris's passion for sharing his experiences in space excited not only people back on Earth, but his fellow astronauts and cosmonauts as well.

people look at astronauts on orbit, and he has brought space flight home to normal people down here." Astronauts are now afraid they'll have to add singing lessons to their training schedule!

While that may be Chris's short-term impact on the space program, it's too early to say what his ultimate legacy to the Canadian space program—and to life on Earth—will be. At 56 years old, he has plenty of time to do much, much more on this planet.

One thing is for sure, though. Future astronauts will find him a tough act to follow.

Logo patches for the combined ISS missions flown by Chris Hadfield, Tom Marshburn, and Roman Romanenko between December 2012 and May 2013. During Expedition 34/35, Chris became a presence on social media, creating a deep bond with his followers back on Earth. He also inspired a sense of awe for both the cosmos and the treasures of our home planet.

This view of North Africa and the Middle East was photographed by Chris Hadfield from the International Space Station and tweeted back to Earth around March 20, 2013. The arrow-shaped mass near the center is the Sinai Peninsula, in Egypt. To the left is the Nile River snaking its way through Egypt to the Mediterranean Sea (at the top of the photo). The dark land area on the other side of the Sinai, curving around the Mediterranean, is Israel. Along with the photo, Chris tweeted back the following caption: "The Nile and the Sinai, to Israel and beyond. One sweeping glance of human history."

Chris Hadfield sending back
to Earth, via Twitter and
Facebook, stunning images of
space and of our planet, along
with him juggling Easter eggs
in zero gravity: Without a
doubt, a hard act to follow!

Chronology

August 29, 1959 Christopher Austin Hadfield born in Sarnia, Ontario, Canada.

1967 Family moves to corn farm in Milton, Ontario.

1969 Watches July 20 Apollo 11 Moon landing on TV; decides he will be an astronaut.

1972 Joins Air Cadets.

1975 Earns glider pilot license.

1976 Earns power pilot license.

1978 Joins Canadian Armed Forces as a student at Royal Roads Military College, then at Royal Military College.

1981 Marries high school sweetheart Helene Walter.

1982 Graduates from military college with bachelor's degree in mechanical engineering.

1983 Takes Basic Jet Training, finishing as top student in his class. Chris and Helene's first son, Kyle, born.

1984–1985 Trains as a fighter jet pilot in Cold Lake, Alberta.

1985 Second son, Evan, born. Chris becomes first CF-18 pilot to intercept a Soviet "Bear" bomber.

1985–1988 Posted to CFB Bagotville; flies with 425 Squadron.

1986 Daughter Kristin born.

1987–1988 Attends U.S. Air Force Test Pilot School at Edwards Air Force Base in California. Graduates as top student in his class.

1988 Posted to Patuxent River Naval Air Station in Maryland.

1991 Named U.S. Navy's Test Pilot of the Year.

1992 January: applies to become an astronaut. May: earns Master of Science degree in aviation systems from University of Tennessee. June: announced as one of six new Canadian astronauts.

1995 November 12: takes off in Space Shuttle *Atlantis* for his first space mission. During eight-day mission, becomes the only Canadian to ever set foot on Russian space station *Mir*. Becomes NASA's chief CAPCOM, or capsule communicator, the voice of Mission Control.

1996 Begins four-year term as Canadian Space Agency's chief astronaut.

2001 April 19: second space mission begins; during this 12-day mission, becomes first Canadian to walk in space. Becomes NASA's Director of Operations at the Yuri Gagarin Cosmonaut Training Center in Russia.

2003 Retires from the Canadian Armed Forces after 25 years of service. Becomes Chief of Robotics for the NASA Astronaut Office at the Johnson Space Center in Houston.

2006 Becomes Chief of International Space Station (ISS) Operations at Johnson Space Center.

2009 Learns he will be commander of International Space Station Expedition 35, to take off in three years.

2010 Commander of NEEMO 14, a NASA undersea mission designed to simulate space experiences.

2012 Along with Tom Marshburn and Roman Romanenko, takes off for Missions 34 and 35 at the ISS on December 19. December 21: Chris and colleagues arrive on the ISS; sends first tweet from the ISS.

2013 March 14: becomes first Canadian to be commander of the ISS. May 12: hands over command of ISS to Pavel Vinogradov; his made-in-space music video of David Bowie's "Space Oddity" is released; departs from the ISS.

May 14: Soyuz capsule carrying Chris, Tom, and Roman back to Earth lands in the steppes of Kazakhstan. (It is late night, March 13, in Houston, when the trio lands in Kazakhstan.) June 10: announces plan to retire from CSA and NASA. July 1: performs for thousands of fans on Canada's Parliament Hill for Canada Day. July 3: last day on the job before he retires. July 5: serves as parade marshal for Calgary Stampede Parade. October: first book, *An Astronaut's Guide to Life on Earth*, is published.

2014 March: presents a TED Talk in Vancouver called *What I Learned from Going Blind in Space*; has been viewed online more than two million times. June: became an Officer of the Order of Canada. September: begins teaching aviation and other classes as part-time professor at University of Waterloo. October: second book, *You Are Here: Around the World in 92 Minutes*, is published.

2015 Announces on Twitter plans to release the first album of music recorded in space. Written by Chris, his brother Dave, and son Evan, the music was recorded with musical collaborators back on Earth while Chris was aboard the ISS in 2013.

Glossary

astrophysicist A scientist who studies the physical characteristics and chemical makeup of stars, planets, and other objects in outer space

camaraderie Friendship and trust among a group of people

cameo appearance A short appearance by someone famous in a play, movie, or other performance

commemorative Made to honor an event or a person

copyright Having to do with the legal right to distribute, publish, produce, or sell a book, song, or other artistic work

cosmonaut The Russian term for an astronaut

cruise missile A low-flying, long-range, highly accurate missile that explodes when it hits its target

cunningly In a clever, tricky sort of way

debrief A review of an event or mission that takes place at its conclusion

deorbited Made to leave orbit on purpose

disoriented Confused, likely to lose one's sense of direction

distance education Getting instruction, usually at a college or university level, without being in the classroom; often done online

graduate degree An advanced university degree

grueling Tiring, difficult, and demanding

honorary doctorate degree A high-level degree from a university that a person is given because of his or her accomplishments, rather than for academic performance

hygiene The practice of keeping yourself and your environment clean to prevent illness

industrial Relating to the manufacturing of goods

lunar module A spacecraft that separates from the main spacecraft to transport astronauts to the surface of the Moon

maneuver A complicated series of movements requiring skill and planning

melancholy Sad and thoughtful

military college A college or university that prepares students for careers in the Armed Forces

module An independent, self-contained segment of a spacecraft

momentum The strength or force something has when it's moving

orb A sphere or globe-shaped body

pas de deux A French, ballet term; literal translation is "steps of two"

Ph.D. An advanced university degree; abbreviation for *"Philosophiae Doctor,"* which is Latin for "Doctor of Philosophy"

photo op Short for "photo opportunity"; a staged scene for media photographers

poignant Capable of making a person feel strong emotion; touching; moving

press conference An event held for members of the media, at which a person or organization makes an announcement or distributes information

primate A group of intelligent mammals sharing certain characteristics that includes apes, monkeys, and humans

public relations Managing the public image of a company or individual by controlling the information that reaches the public

quarantined Isolated from other people

recruit To persuade someone to join or work for a group, such as a company or the military

resolution A decision or promise to do something

risk factor Anything that increases a person's likelihood of getting an illness or injury

savvy An understanding or knowledge of how to do something

scenario A sequence of events; a possible outcome

Soviet Union A former nation made up of a group of republics in parts of eastern Europe and northern Asia. The Soviet Union dissolved in 1991, creating a group of independent nations out of its former republics, including Russia, Ukraine, Kazakhstan, and Georgia

Soyuz A type of spacecraft, created by the Soviet Union in the 1960s and still in use by Russia today

space race A period of time, generally considered to be from 1955 through the early-to-mid-1970s, when the United States and the Soviet Union competed to put satellites and people in orbit and on the Moon

squadron A fleet of airplanes, boats, or other military vehicles and personnel

transformational Life-changing

ultrasound A medical test that uses high-frequency sound waves to produce images of structures within a person or animal's body

Further Information

Books

Hadfield, Chris. *An Astronaut's Guide to Life on Earth: What Going to Space Taught Me About Ingenuity, Determination, and Being Prepared for Anything*. New York: Little, Brown and Company, 2013; Toronto: Random House Canada, 2013.

Hadfield, Chris. *You Are Here: Around the World in 92 Minutes: Photographs from the International Space Station*. Toronto: Random House Canada, 2014.

McDonald, Bob. *Canadian Spacewalkers: Hadfield, MacLean and Williams Remember the Ultimate High Adventure*. Madeira Park, BC: Douglas & McIntyre, 2014.

Videos

What I Learned from Going Blind in Space. Ted Talks, March 2014. In this 18-minute Ted Talk, Chris Hadfield speaks about spiders, fears, and floating in space. The lecture also features photos of Earth from space, videos of a space shuttle launch and a Soyuz landing, and a little musical performance. Watch online: **ted.com/talks/chris_hadfield_what_i_learned_from_going_blind_in_space#t-5396**

In Canada. Dave Hadfield, Chris Hadfield, July 2014. For Canada Day (July 1) 2014, the Hadfield brothers "set out to make the most Canadian music video ever." This five-minute song is the result. Watch online: **youtube.com/watch?v=zuVsHt3rBnc&feature=youtu.be**

The Man, the Mission and the Music. CBC Television, December 2012. In this segment of the science program *Quirks & Quarks*, Chris takes host Bob McDonald on a tour of a mock-up of the ISS before his launch to the real one. Watch online: **cbc.ca/player/Shows/ID/2317307306/**

Websites

chrishadfield.ca
This official website is a great place to start for photos, videos, news, and information about Chris. You can view dozens of his ISS videos here, along with more than 200 photos he took of, and from, space.

nasa.gov/audience/forkids/kidsclub/flash/
spaceplace.nasa.gov/
NASA has two websites for young people. The Kids' Club has activities and games relating to spacecraft, astronauts, and the ISS. The Space Place looks at those things, along with broader subjects, including the Sun, the solar system, technology, and weather.

zenpencils.com/comic/106-chris-hadfield-an-astronauts-advice/
In March 2013, Australian cartoonist Gavin Aung Than turned some of Chris Hadfield's words of wisdom into a series of comic panels. Gaving's website, Zen Pencils, features cartoon illustrations of inspiring quotes from many people.

spacekids.co.uk/learn/
In the "Learn About Space" pages of the Spacekids website, you will find short, illustrated articles on everything from spacesuits to space ships, and from eating in space to becoming an astronaut.

thekidshouldseethis.com/tagged/space/
This site features 134 videos about space. You can take *A 25-Minute Tour of the International Space Station*, or learn *How Astronauts Put on Space Suits*, or simply gaze at *Stunning Views of Earth from the International Space Station*. Some of Chris Hadfield's videos appear on this website, as does the fun, but educational, *Spacesuit Ballet*. Take some time and explore!

worldspaceflight.com/bios/index.php
If you're interested in facts, figures, statistics, and a who's-who of astronauts and cosmonauts, check out this website. You can search for space travelers by nationality, by name, or by the order in which they flew. You will find statistics related to spacewalking, a list of who is currently in space, and a timeline of international space travel.

Index

About the Author

Diane Dakers was born and raised in Toronto and now makes her home in Victoria, British Columbia. Diane has been a newspaper, magazine, television, and radio journalist since 1991. She is a lifelong stargazer who, like millions of other Earthlings, caught @Cmdr_Hadfield fever in 2012–2013.